LANTERNS & LANCES

Books by James Thurber

James Thurber

LANTERNS
& LANCES

HARPER & BROTHERS, PUBLISHERS, NEW YORK

TO

ROSE ALGRANT, a lady with a lantern, who lights the pathways of all of us lucky enough to live where she lives, this book is dedicated with love, wonder, and gratitude.

Contents

Acknowledgments

"The Saving Grace," "The Porcupines in the Artichokes," and "The Case for Comedy" originally appeared in the *Atlantic Monthly,* and "My Senegalese Birds and Siamese Cats" and "Such a Phrase as Drifts Through Dreams" in *Holiday.*

"Magical Lady" was first printed in the Sunday *New York Times.*

"Here Come the Dolphins" and "The New Vocabularianism" are from *Punch.* "The Darlings at the Top of the Stairs" was published by the English magazine *The Queen,* and also appeared in *Harper's.* The *Saturday Review* printed "Come Across with the Facts" and *Suburbia Today* "A Moment with Mandy" and "How to Get Through the Day."

"How the Kooks Crumble" appears in print here for the first time.

"The Duchess and the Bugs" was a response to an award given in 1953 by the Ohioana Library Association. It was later published in brochure form by the World Publishing Company.

The other ten pieces in this book first appeared in *The New Yorker.*

Foreword

"Don't you think that things are getting better?" a woman asked me not long ago at a party.

"Madam," I replied, in my courtly, but slightly edged fashion, "things will take care of themselves. What I am interested in is people."

By people she thought that I meant persons, and she began rattling off facts and figures about sundry marriages and divorces of Hollywood celebrities and total strangers. In this dreary field of vital statistics I am not at home, and I began throwing forward passes wildly, about the state of the Union, world affairs, and a few recent books. As usually happens when I encounter ladies at parties, this got me nowhere. "I have reason to believe," said my companion, "that my fourteen-year-old daughter has a bottle of vodka hidden somewhere in the house."

I didn't know what to say to that, so I didn't say anything, which is rather unusual for me at a party. She looked at me sharply. "You're much too serious nowadays," she said. "What has made you so lubugrious all of a sudden?"

I trust that this collection of pieces will prove that I have not become, at sixty-six going on fifty, as one friend of mine gallantly put it, completely "lubugrious." Many things, or rather people and ideas, are dealt with here in what I hope is a humorous vein, for, as I keep pointing out, humor in a living culture must not be put away in the attic with the flag, but should be flaunted, like the flag, bravely. Every time is a time for comedy in a world of tension that would languish without it. But I cannot confine myself to lightness in a period of human life that demands light, and I have been heartened to observe that light, as a symbol of the courageous heart and the upward mind, appears more and more often in the titles and in the contents of books in all fields.

Much of what follows, therefore, is my own attempt, in my little corner of the struggle, to throw a few lantern beams here and there. But I also cast a few lances at the people and the ideas that have disturbed me, and I make no apology for their seriousness. Some were written in anger, which has become one of the necessary virtues, and, if there is a touch of the "lubugrious" in certain pieces, the perceptive reader will also detect, I like to think, a basic and indestructible thread of hope.

Swinburne once wrote, in a famous poem, that he had

been set free from too much love of living, and from hope
and fear. The man who finds such false freedom nowadays has withdrawn from life, and might as well spend
the rest of his time playing checkers or throwing darts.

We all know that, as the old adage has it, "It is later than
you think." I touch on that theme myself, as every writer
who can think must, but I also say occasionally: "It is
lighter than you think." In this light, let's not look back
in anger, or forward in fear, but around in awareness.

J. T.

West Cornwall
Connecticut

LANTERNS
& LANCES

1

How to Get
Through the Day

"How do you get through the day?" a woman out in Iowa has asked me in a letter. I can't tell whether she wants help in getting through her own day, or whether she has made a wager with somebody that I don't get through my own day at all, but somehow contrive to get *around* it. The truth is that I do get through the day and, if it will benefit anybody, I shall be glad to state how I manage it. It might be simpler to put my method in the form of rules.

One: Never answer a telephone that rings before breakfast. It is sure to be one of three types of persons that is calling: a strange man in Minneapolis who has been up all night and is phoning collect; a salesman who wants to come over and demonstrate a new, patented combination

Dictaphone and music box that also cleans rugs; or a woman out of one's past. Just let the phone ring. The woman would be sure to say:

"This is Thelma Terwilliger. What are you going to *do* about me?" If you talk to her before your orange juice and coffee, or even afterward, for that matter, you will never get through the day. Professors Radnor and Grube, in their monumentally depressing treatise *The Female of the*

Species, list a total of 1,113 possible involvements with a woman, all but eight of them ranging from the untoward to the inextricable.

Two: If you want to keep your breakfast down, do not read the front page, or any page, of the morning newspaper. Fifteen years ago the late Professor Herman Allen Miller of Ohio State University wrote me that, out there, no news was the only good news. He would be saddened, but not surprised, to learn that nowadays no news is the only good news anywhere. It is better to dip into *The Last*

Days of Pompeii than to peruse the morning paper at breakfast, but what I do is turn on WQXR for classical or semiclassical music, or WPAT for popular music out of the late lamented American past—such songs, for example, as "Whispering," "Sleepy Time Gal," "Sunny," and "Honey, Honey, Bless Your Heart." (If you have been foolish enough to talk with Thelma, the last two songs will probably become "Money," and "Money, Money, Bless Your Heart.") One morning, by mistake, I got another station than WPAT and listened, relaxed, to a recording of "People Will Say We're in Love," sung by Alfred Drake and Joan Roberts, when suddenly it terminated and a young detergent voice began yelling:

"Don't knock rock 'n' roll, it's a rockin' good way to mess around and fall in love." What have we done to deserve this? Or should I say, what have we done not to deserve it?

Three: Avoid the ten-o'clock news on the radio, at all costs. It is always confined to disasters—automobile accidents involving seventeen cars, the fatal stabbing of a fourteen-year-old girl by her twelve-year-old sweetheart, attacks on young mothers in Brooklyn basements, and riotous demonstrations by fifteen thousand students in Graustark. It is comforting, in a vaguely uneasy way, to realize that American students do not engage in political demonstrations, but reserve their passions for panty raids, jazz festivals, and the hanging of football coaches in effigy.

Four: Do not open the morning mail when it arrives if you are alone in the house. If I am alone when my mail arrives, around eleven o'clock, I wait for my wife to get back from the hairdresser. If she says, "God!" or "Oh, no!" after glancing at a letter, I hastily tell her to send it on to our lawyer or our agent, without reading it to me. I now get about twelve letters every morning, and she is happy if not more than two of them call for wedding presents. About seven of the twelve always call for something, and you ought to consider yourself lucky that you are not me. I am asked to read something, to write something, to send something, to do something, to explain something, or to go somewhere. These letters invariably begin like this: "I realize that you are a very busy man, but . . ." and they always end: "Thanks for your time and trouble." I am pleased to report that at least two letters every day are intelligent, warm, and even humorous, and that they almost invariably come from American wives and mothers unknown to me, who frequently say, "I love you." This cheers me up enormously, until I begin thinking about Thelma Terwilliger again.

Five: Some years ago a distinguished American woman physician recommended "a nap after lunch and a nip before dinner." I myself do not recommend the nap after lunch, except for infants. My researches among those who have tried it show that 80 per cent of the males and 100 per cent of the females just lie there wide-eyed, strumming the headboard with their fingers and/or, as the lawyers say, moaning low. Among the thoughts that keep Americans awake are—but why should I list them, sleepless reader, when you know what they are as well as I do?

As for the nip before dinner, I'm all for it, unless it

leads to a nipping that doesn't end until after three o'clock in the morning. Speaking of tranquillizers, which everybody always is, I do not turn to Miltown, but to Milton, and to some of the other bards sublime, and a few of the humbler poets. Because of the distressing process of mental association, however, poetry is not always a help. The other morning, for example, I got to Edna St. Vincent Millay's "There isn't a train I wouldn't take, no matter where it's going" when it suddenly turned into "There isn't a train that I can take, no matter where I'm going." This disturbing paraphrase grew out of a seven-week period of travel in the Middle West last winter, during which I had to be driven by car from Columbus, Ohio, to Detroit because the only train out of the Ohio capital for the great Michigan city leaves at 4 A.M. I also found it simpler to be driven from Detroit to Cleveland, since railroad transportation in the Middle West has regressed to about where it was at the time of Custer's Last Stand.

The trouble with turning to verse while nipping before dinner, especially in a public place like the lobby of the Hotel Algonquin, is that one is likely to grow irritable, or even bitter, instead of leaning back and relaxing in one's chair. A playwright I know, who tried repeating lines of Longfellow to himself in the Algonquin lobby at six o'clock one evening, was abruptly impelled, while nipping his fourth martini, to accost a strange lady and proclaim, "*I* say the struggle naught availeth, madam," after which he turned to a male stranger and snarled, "Life is but an empty dream, Mac." He then returned to his own chair. All of a sudden he spotted a poet across the lobby, and he was upon him in a moment, saying, "Hell with thee, blythe spirit, bard thou never wert." When the rude fellow later told me, proudly, what he had said, I could only snarl, on my own fourth nip before dinner, "I am glad you did not once see Shelley plain, and did not stop and talk to him."

Six: This brings us to the dinner hour and the problem

of getting through *that*. Here everybody has to work out his own system of getting his dinner down, and keeping it down. Dinner-table conversation should be selected with great care nowadays since the first seventeen subjects that spring to mind are likely to be gloomy, running from the muddle-fuddle of international relations to the dangers of cholesterol and di-ester stilvesterol, and if you don't know what they are, I'm not going to tell you. My wife and I, Monday through Friday, usually dine in our own home with thirteen and a half million and one Americans, the thirteen and a half million members of the C.I.O.-A.F. of L. who sponsor the commentator Edward P. Morgan on WABC at seven P.M., and Mr. Morgan himself. The good strong voice of Elmer Davis is no longer heard in the land, but Mr. Morgan carries on ably in his stead, with the same intelligence, devotion to American ideals, courage, and wit. One night, during Christmas week of 1959, he discussed the lavish, expensive, and empty celebration of Holy Week and said, "We seem to forget that Christ was born in a manger and not in the Bethlehem-Hilton." It is a thought to remember.

Seven: Tender is the night no more, as we all know, especially the summer night, and when it falls, I always think of Robert Benchley's provocative title, "What to Do When It Gets Dark." Most married couples, I have found out, totter to the television set and turn it on, but I would rather read something restful instead, like *The Naked and the Dead*. It is perhaps enough to say of the Westerns, that endless series of morbid discharges, that they inspired a certain little girl's definition of a hung jury as "twelve men hanging from a tree." As for the police bang-bangs, they seem more and more given over to the theory that most killers in our society are women, so that as soon as a demure wife or ex-wife appears on the scene, you can be pretty sure that she did it. She usually confesses, at the end, in a quiet voice, saying, simply, "Yes, Lieutenant, I killed him."

This may not give *you* the creeps but it gives *me* the creeps.

Eight: This brings us to beddy-bye. Well, good night, and I pray the Lord your soul to keep. My own nocturnal problem in the summertime consists of flying creatures, great big June bugs, or bang-sashes. One of them banged the sash of the window nearest my bed around midnight in July, and I leaped out of sleep and out of bed. "It's just a bat," said my wife reassuringly, and I sighed with relief. "Thank God for that," I said. "I thought it was a human being."

2

Midnight at
Tim's Place

"Old sundials used to boast, in Latin, and I suppose a few in quiet gardens here and there still do, *'Horas non numero nisi serenas'*—'I count serene hours only.'"

"*Et pourquoi pas?*" my wife asked vaguely.

It was our first night home after six months in Europe, and the hour at Tim's was late, and more melancholy than serene. We had just heard of the decline of several friends when the stranger with the empty highball glass and the Latin phrase hopped our table.

"My name is Warren Kirkfield," he said unconvincingly, holding out a damp right hand.

"I bet his real name is Chase or Psst," said the pretty young woman on my left. I didn't know who she was, or how she had got there. The newcomer ignored this.

"Sit down," I said unwarmly. "Urge up a footstool, loosen your stays, saucer your Scotch."

"Don't be so cruel," said my wife, moving over so Kirkfield could sit next to her, across the table from me and the fair unknown. "Maybe he has a right to be sad—it's a free country. Maybe you can't always be *everything* in it, but you can be that."

"No politics," said the young woman, with the faintest of hiccups.

"My name is Keith Maitland," I lied, "and this is my wife, the former Geraldine Spinney. The lady on my left is a nameless waif out of the night, a poor windlestraw on the stream of time."

"Ah thought you-all was Bing Crosby," said the windlestraw, in a fake Dixie that was not too bad for one in her cups. Fake Dixie always enchants me after midnight. I prayed God to keep my hand off her knee.

"Everybody is in the groove tonight," my wife explained.

"Everybody is just another Gabriel Heatter."

Suddenly we all had a fresh drink. "How are you, Bing?" asked Kirkfield, clinking his glass against mine.

"*Non sum qualis eram sub regno bony Sinatra*," I said quickly, having waited for years to wedge that line in somewhere.

"You finally made it," my wife said, for she knows all my lines, wedged and unwedged.

"You're just a goddam kissing bug," the windlestraw told Kirkfield. "I saw you." She turned to me. "I can't leave him alone a minute but what he's bending some girl over backward. This one had glasses and too much teeth."

"I was being a gentleman," protested Kirkfield. "The lady had something in her eye."

"What was it?" asked Mrs. Kirkfield, for it was unquestionably she. "A roguish twinkle?"

"I came here to tell these charming people a sad story, not to refight the war between the sexes," Kirkfield said.

"Oh, my God! Not that story again," said his wife.

I had lost interest in her knee. "Go ahead, Maitland," I said.

"Just call me plain Keith," he murmured.

"The people at the next table must think they are losing their minds," my wife put in.

"Or ours," Mrs. Kirkfield amended.

"Well, then," Kirkfield began, "I was on the edge of a nervous crackup last summer, for the usual variety of reasons—fear of death, fear of life, fear of the inhuman being. Also, I had just become forty-one, and realized that I only had nineteen years to live before I would begin to cackle."

11

"I won't be there," said his wife's voice, from inside her highball glass. "He'll be bald as a beagle and his back will hurt and he'll babble about his conquex."

"Quests," my wife corrected her.

"You can say that again," said Mrs. Kirkfield.

"There was only one person I wanted to see, wanted to talk to," Kirkfield went on. "The greatest symbol of security in my life, the man who could pull me back from the doors of Hell, my old philosophy professor, Dr. Pensinger. I had not seen him for five years, but for nearly twenty we had exchanged postcards at Christmas and, because it amused him—you know how professors are— on Nietzsche's birthday."

"I got to have more whiskey to get through this again," said his wife, and we got more whiskey.

"Everybody, in college and afterward, turned to Dr.

Pensinger for inspiration and consolation," her husband went on. "He had, and still has, some piece of unique philosophy for each special case. 'You can keep a stiff upper lip, and smile, too,' and 'Don't let that chip on your shoulder be your only reason for walking erect.' We always left Dr. Pensinger's study with a high heart and renewed hope."

"I just won't be there, that's all," his wife cut in. "Let him stomp his cane and yell his head off, for all I care. Give me a man like Gary Cooper or Harpo Marx, who doesn't talk for God's sake all the time."

I touched her glass with mine, and said, "Here's something in your eye, I hope."

"Much he'd care if you did," she said.

"Well, last summer, when I got the galloping jumps, I decided to call on Dr. Pensinger and see if he could pull me out of it," Kirkfield said. "He lives in a charming house in Riverdale, and I drove up there one Sunday afternoon. His wife opened the door, and said, 'We don't need anything today.' Before she could shut the door, I told her who I was and why I was there, and she said Dr. Pensinger was in his study and I could just go on in, and so I did. It was a terrifying visit. He had not changed a bit. He did not even seem a day older than the last time I had met him and listened to his cheering words. The same thoughtful blue eyes, the same reassuring smile, the same gentle voice." Kirkfield took a great gulp of his highball.

"Then what was terrifying about the visit?" I asked.

Kirkfield lit a cigarette. "He was wearing two hats," he said. There was a long pause.

13

"In his study?" I asked.

"*Two* hats?" my wife asked, putting her realistic finger on the more incongruous fact.

"Two hats," Kirkfield repeated. "They were both gray felt hats, one on top of the other. The terrifying thing was that he didn't say anything about them. He just sat there with two hats on, trying to cheer me up."

"I always say you can have too much philosophy," Mrs. Kirkfield said. "It isn't good for you. It's disorganizing. Everybody's got to wake up sometime feeling that everything is terrible, because it is."

"Couldn't you have said, 'Pardon me, but you seem to be wearing two hats'?" my wife wanted to know.

"No, I couldn't," said Kirkfield. "I don't even remember how I got out of there. I had the chattering jitters. His wife showed me to the door, and said, 'Did he buy anything? If he did, I'll simply send it back when it arrives.'"

I thought it was time for another drink. We had all finished our last one very quickly.

"We never know what's going to happen to us," my wife said.

"I don't care i ɪy husband wears *three* hats," his wife said. "I won't be there."

I had a sudden frightening vision of walking about the city in a few years, wearing only one shoe. Even my best friends, I realized, wouldn't mention it. I thought it was time to go home now, and stood up. My wife and I left the Kirkfields sitting there with four drinks, since we had not touched our new ones.

Tim helped me on with my overcoat, and handed me

14

my hat, and we started to the door. One of the waiters came running after me, and handed me a hat. "You left this the last time you were here," he said. "You went away without a hat that night."

"Don't you dare!" my wife said, but I put the hat he gave me on top of the one I was wearing, and we went out into the street, and I whistled for a taxi. Pretty soon, one drove up and stopped, but when the driver saw that I was wearing two hats, he said, "Not in this cab, Jack." He was about to drive off when my wife opened the door and got in. "I'll see you at the Algonquin," she said, "if you get that far."

I stood there for a long while, and it began to rain. I walked back to the hotel in the rain.

3

The Darlings at the Top of the Stairs

Childhood used to end with the discovery that there is no Santa Claus. Nowadays, it too often ends when the child gets his first adult, the way Hemingway got his first rhino, with the difference that the rhino was charging Hemingway, whereas the adult is usually running from the child. This has brought about a change in the folklore and mythology of the American home, and of the homes of other offspring-beleaguered countries. The dark at the top of the stairs once shrouded imaginary bears that lay in wait for tiny tots, but now parents, grandparents, and other grown relatives are afraid there may be a little darling lurking in the shadows, with blackjack, golf club, or .32-caliber automatic.

The worried psychologists, sociologists, anthropologists, and other ologists, who jump at the sound of every back-fire or slammed door, have called our present jeopardy a "child-centered culture." Every seven seconds a baby is born in the United States, which means that we produce, every two hours, approximately five companies of infantry. I would say this amounts to a child-overwhelmed culture, but I am one of those who do not intend to surrender meekly and unconditionally. There must be a bright side to this menacing state of civilization, and if somebody will snap on his flashlight, we'll take a look around for it.

More has been written about the child than about any other age of man, and it is perhaps fortunate that the literature is now so extensive a child would have become twenty-one before its parents could get through half the books on how to bring it up. The trouble with the "child expert" is that he is so often a dedicated, or desiccated, expository writer and lecturer, and the tiny creative talents he attempts to cope with are beyond him. Margaret Mead, the American anthropologist, is an exception, for she realizes the dangers inherent in twisting infantile creativity into the patterns of adult propriety, politeness, and conformity. Let us glance at a few brief examples of creative literature in the very young, for which they should have been encouraged, not admonished.

The small girl critic who wrote, "This book tells me more about penguins than I wanted to know," has a technique of clarity and directness that might well be studied by the so-called mature critics of England and the United States, whose tendency, in dealing with books about

17

penguins or anything else, is to write long autobiographical rambles.

Then there was the little American girl who was asked by her teacher to write a short story about her family. She managed it in a single true and provocative sentence: "Last night my daddy didn't come home at all." I told this to a five-year-old moppet I know and asked her if she could do as well, and she said, "Yes," and she did. Her short story, in its entirety, went like this: "My daddy doesn't take anything with him when he goes away except a nightie and whiskey."

I am known to parents as a disruptive force, if not indeed a naughty influence, upon my small colleagues in the field of imaginative writing. When Sally, aged four, told me, "I want to be a ghost," her mother said quickly, "No, you don't," and I said, "Yes, she does. Let her be a ghost. Maybe she will become another W. E. Henley, who wrote, 'And the world's a ghost that gleams, flickers, vanishes away.'"

"Who is W. E. Henley?" the child's mother asked uneasily.

"Wilhelmina Ernestine Henley," I explained. "A poet who became a ghost."

Her mother said she didn't want Sally to become a poet or a ghost, but a good wife and mother.

Finally, there was Lisa, aged five, whose mother asked her to thank my wife for the peas we had sent them the day before from our garden. "I thought the peas were awful, I wish you and Mrs. Thurber was dead, and I hate trees," said Lisa, thus conjoining in one creative splurge the nursery rhyme about pease porridge cold, the basic plot sense of James M. Cain, and Birnam wood moving upon Dunsinane. Lisa and I were the only unhorrified persons in the room when she brought this out. We knew that her desire to get rid of her mother and my wife at one fell swoop was a pure device of creative literature. As I explained to the two doomed ladies later, it is important to let your little daughters and sons kill you off figuratively, because this is a natural infantile urge that cannot safely be channeled into amenity or what Henry James called "the twaddle of graciousness." The child that is scolded or punished for its natural human desire to destroy is likely to turn later to the blackjack, the golf club, or the .32-caliber automatic.

The tiny twaddler of ungraciousness has my blessing, as you can see. You can also see that I am mainly concerned with the incipient, or burgeoning, creativity of the female child. This is because I am more interested in Thurber's theory of Elaine Vital, the female life force, than in Bergson's theory of Elan Vital, the masculine life force, which it seems to me is all he isolated. Elaine Vital, if properly directed—that is, let alone—may become the hope of the future. God knows we have enough women writers (at least one too many, if you ask me), but I believe they are the product of a confined and constrained infantile creativity. Being females, they have turned to the pen and the typewriter, instead of the blackjack, golf club, and .32-caliber automatic.

Boys are perhaps beyond the range of anybody's sure understanding, at least when they are between the ages of eighteen months and ninety years. They have got us into the human quandary, dilemma, plight, predicament, pickle, mess, pretty pass, and kettle of fish in which we now find ourselves. Little boys are much too much for me at my age, for it is they who have taken over the American home, physically. They are in charge of running everything, usually into the ground.

Most American parents will not answer the telephone when it rings, but will let a little boy do it. Telephone

operators, I have been informed, now frequently say to a mumbling toddler, "Is there anyone older than you in the house?" Many of the tradespeople and artisans I deal with, or try to, in my part of Connecticut, go in for this form of evasionism. A small male child will pick up the receiver and burble into the transmitter. In this way urgency, or even crisis, is met with baby talk, or prattle tattle. The fact that my plumbing has let go or a ceiling is falling down is reduced, in this new system of non-communication, to a tiny, halting, almost inaudible recital of what happened to a teddy bear, or why cereal is not good with sliced bananas and should be thrown at Daddy. The tradesman or artisan and his wife are spared the knowledge of a larger disaster at the expense of the nerves and mental balance of the caller. I shall set down here an exasperating personal experience in this area of obfuscation.

"Oo tiss?" a tiny voice demanded when I called the plumber one day.

"This is Tanta Twaus," I said, "and Tanta Twaus won't give you any Twissmas pwesents this Twissmas if you do not put Mommy or Daddy on the other end of this doddam apparatus."

"Appawana?" asked the tiny voice. At this point his mother, like a woman in transport and on her third martini, grabbed up the receiver.

"He said, 'Appomattox,' didn't he?" she cried. "Isn't that wonderful?"

"Madam," I said, chilling the word, "the answer to the question I just put to your son is Waterloo, not Appomattox. The next voice you hear will be that of me, dying in the flood of broken pipes and the rubble of fallen ceilings." And I slammed up the receiver.

Ours is indeed a child-centered culture in the sense that the little boys have got me squarely centered in their gun sights. I shall continue to urge on the little girls who hate trees, are indifferent to penguins, envy Banquo, wish Mother were with the angels, and can read Daddy like a book. What you are going to do, I don't know, but I advise you to keep glancing over your shoulder, and look out for the darlings at the top of the stairs.

4

The Porcupines
in the Artichokes

"I have writers the way other people have mice," a disturbed hostess has written me. "What can I do to keep them from arguing, fighting, and throwing highball glasses after dinner? One doesn't dare mention names, such as Herman Melville and Harold Loeb, or the fight is on. What would you suggest?"

Well, now, it isn't easy to entertain writers and have any fun. You might begin by saying, over the first cocktail, "I don't want any writers to be mentioned this evening." Do not make the mistake of adding, "From Washington Irving to Jack Kerouac," because that would instantly precipitate an argument about Washington Irving and Jack Kerouac. You might begin by saying, "The porcupines are getting our artichokes." This could, of course, lead to literary wrangling and jangling, but everything is a calculated risk when writers are present, even "My grandfather almost married a Pawnee woman," or "I wonder if you gentlemen would help me put the handle back on my icebox." A writer, of course, can turn anything at all into a literary discussion, and it might be better not to say anything about anything.

I myself have found, or rather my wife has found, that you can sometimes keep writers from fighting by getting them into some kind of pencil-and-paper game. You could say, for example, "There are thirty-seven given names and nicknames, male and female, in the word 'miracle.' I want you all to see how many you can find." This almost always takes up a good hour, during which the writers are mercifully silent.

My wife, during a party in August, when writers are at

their worst, brought out the pencils and paper and said, "I want you all to write down the names of as many animals and birds as you can think of with a double 'o' in their names." This worked fine for about half an hour, during which the literary men wrote down: moose, goose, mongoose, raccoon, baboon, loon, rook, coot, spoonbill, kangaroo, cockatoo, rooster, poodle, bloodhound, woodchuck, woodpecker, woodcock, whippoorwill, and cuckoo.

The trouble started, as my wife should have known it would, when the papers were gathered up and the scoring began. Every writer, in a room full of writers, wants to be the best, and the judge, or umpire, or referee is soon overwhelmed and shouted down like a chickadee trying to take charge of a caucus of crows. Nobody can ever remember exactly what happened at any drinking party invaded and taken over by writers, because, as the bowl continues to flow, their eloquence and invention take on the sharp edge of temper and cussedness. My wife gave up the hopeless task of scoring and turned it over to a lawyer guest when the question of the validity of habitat names set all the crows to cawing at once. It was decided that brook trout, moor hen, stool pigeon, and the like were out. Then there turned up, on this paper and that, what the lawyer, raising his voice, called behavior names— whooping crane, which was allowed after near fisticuffs, hoot owl, which also made it, and moo cow, which was shouted down, along with brood mare. The lawyer-judge, full of Scotch and a love of definition, tried to put into separate categories saber-toothed tiger, hooded falcon, smooth-haired fox terrier, hookworm and bookworm, hoop

24

snake, and coon dog, and it was soon evident that the task of arbiter was too much for him.

There are always two or three writers, in this kind of game, who deliberately louse things up by taking and holding an untenable position. One of these obstinate fellows had written down pool shark, and another had come up with booze hound, and they defended their stand on the ground that my wife, in the beginning, had not stipulated *real* animals and birds. The shouting about this died down when micro-organism turned up on the paper of a stuffy textbook writer, who defended it on the ground that a double "o" is a double "o" whether hyphenated or not. Everybody turned on him, and somebody threw an ash tray.

At this point my wife drew me aside, which isn't easy to do at a yelling party, since I am a writer, too, and told me, "You'll simply have to get them to singing." I tried to get them to singing, but it was no good, because the whooping-crane man and the brook-trout man suddenly began attacking each other's books, viewpoint, style, and implementation. In a sense, the crane of whooping crane and the brook of brook trout saved the situation, if wreckage can be saved by further wreckage. All of a moment a whooping literary argument was on. It concerned the merits and demerits of Rupert Brooke, Stephen Crane, Tennyson's "The Brook" and Tennyson himself, Hart Crane, and Bret Harte; also *The Heart of the Matter, The Heart Is a Lonely Hunter,* and *The Death of the Heart,* thus involving Graham Greene, Carson McCullers, Elizabeth Bowen, Kenneth Grahame, *The Wind in the*

Willows, Gone With the Wind, Kenneth Tynan, Kenneth Burke, *A Biography of Kit Carson,* Burke's Speech on Conciliation with the Colonies, Marc Connelly, Mark Sabre, *If Winter Comes,* Robert Frost, W. H. Auden, J. D. Salinger, *J. B.,* A. E. Housman, AE, A. J. Liebling, *B. F.'s Daughter,* and, if my memory serves, Herman Melville, Harold Loeb, Washington Irving, and Jack Kerouac.

That night three highball glasses, two friendships, and a woman's heart were broken. There is really only one safe rule for a hostess to go by. Do not ask writers to your house, especially in the summer, and in three other seasons of the year—spring, autumn, and winter.

I was going to end my advice to hostesses on that wintry note, but after tossing and turning in bed for two or three minutes one night, which is all I can do at my age without falling asleep, I decided that I had not been helpful enough to the lady in distress who wrote me. She should, then, hide any flat package a writer brings to her party. It is likely to contain a long-playing record which he intends to plop on her phonograph when everybody else wants to argue, and there are things worse than writers' arguing, such as a recording, in Ooglala Sioux, of a group of Indian squaws chanting in an endless monotone, with a background of tom-toms, a dirge mourning the miscarriage of a chief's daughter or daughter-in-law. If it isn't that, it will be a recording of "The Waste Land" in Gaelic, or a recitation of "Evangeline" by the writer's five-year-old niece. Don't let your writer guests get their teeth into poetry, for God's sake. Prose is bad enough, but poetry is worse. Somebody is sure to misquote "Under a spreading chestnut tree," by changing the "a" to "the," and the hecklers will be at him like dogs on a bone. Somebody will then bet somebody else that he can't correctly finish "The light that never was . . ." and he will be right, because the challenged man will say, "on land or sea," when it is really "on sea or land." The hostess should conceal all flat packages and return them later, the later the better.

It is high time that a note of hope, or at least of wan cheerfulness, creep into this discourse. Don't get the idea that writers never agree about anything, because they do, approximately twice during the course of an eight-hour evening. Their form of agreement goes roughly like this: "You are right, you are right, you are absolutely right! The trouble is, you don't have the vaguest idea *why* you are." The writer who is thus agreed with will, of course, disagree with the agreer, like this: "You are completely wrong, and so was I. It is remarkable how you always reveal the weakness of a point by insisting that it is well taken." Here the point, whatever it may have been, is lost sight of in an exchange of what might be called abstract double talk, or backfiring Dada. Now nobody in the room knows what the writers are not talking about, including the two men themselves.

My experience of writers at parties goes back to the year that *Jurgen* was published and has been confined to endless talkers born between the years 1885 and 1905, the wives of some of whom have not got in more than ninety words edgewise since 1922—at parties, that is. When the writer husband is hung over, the wife is allowed to talk, and she often does, though knowing full well that her spouse isn't paying any attention. The literary men roughly in my age group become more articulate, and less coherent, as the years go on, but their age does not keep them away from parties. Now and then those who are in their sixties or seventies confuse *Spoon River Anthology* with *Of Time and the River,* but otherwise it is hard to tell them from the younger men.

Among the American writers I have stayed up with all night were—to name only those who are, alas, no longer with us—Robert Benchley, Heywood Broun, Scott Fitzgerald, Thomas Wolfe, and Sinclair Lewis. Benchley was, as everybody knows who knew him, the Great Companion, who often talked about the mystery and lure of heaven when the bright stars were waning. Broun was usually in some area of politics, justice, and fair play. Once, around two in the morning, he asked me not to cross a picket line that had been set up in front of "21," and I had to tell him that that was where we were. "Under the circumstances then," he said in that unforgettable voice, "I think we should have another drink." Fitzgerald talked about the dear dead past, the Unattained and the Unattainable, for he was the romantic to the end, and the farthest removed of all male writers from such subjects as the conquest of an old-time movie actress in the back seat of a Hupmobile in the year when Teddy Roosevelt stood at Armageddon and battled for the Lord. Wolfe discoursed for twelve hours about love, and writing (his own), and Carolina. Lewis was all over the written and unwritten areas of his time, and went in for some excellent mimicry of his colleagues. All these unforgettable nights except one —I met the wondrous Sinclair Lewis in Bermuda—were spent in New York City. In London, the British writers have a strange way of going home from a party before daybreak, and the one whose early departure I always most regret is Compton Mackenzie, as good an actor and imitator as he is a writer, whose impersonation of Wordsworth I would go three thousand miles to see, and have more than once.

It was the late incomparable John McNulty who had the perfect answer to the problems of the writer-beleaguered hostess. McNulty was a piano-playing man, and he once said, "The thing to do in mixed company is play 'Dear Old Girl.' " He would stop the fight about Jim Tully or James Branch Cabell by going to the piano and sliding into "Dear Old Girl" in his famous silent-movie-theatre style, and every guy in the room between the ages of eighteen and eighty would lean on the piano and join in the chorus. That undying song, first published in 1903, I think, leads naturally into "Let Me Call You Sweetheart," "I Want a Girl Just Like the Girl," "Down by the Old Mill Stream," and all the rest, with no space for rock 'n' roll, or rockers and rollers, or for the voices of writers raised in argument instead of melody.

Let me, in conclusion, assure the distraught hostess that some of my best friends are writers, and adjure her, for God's sake, not to bring them and me together at a party at her house. We write such lovely letters to each other, it would be a shame to spoil it.

5

The Spreading
"*You* Know"

The latest blight to afflict the spoken word in the United States is the rapidly spreading reiteration of the phrase "*you* know." I don't know just when it began moving like a rainstorm through the language, but I tremble at its increasing garbling of meaning, ruining of rhythm, and drumming upon my hapless ears. One man, in a phone conversation with me last summer, used the phrase thirty-four times in about five minutes, by my own count; a young matron in Chicago got seven "*you* knows" into one wavy sentence, and I have also heard it as far west as Denver, where an otherwise charming woman at a garden party in August said it almost as often as a whip-poorwill says, "Whippoorwill." Once, speaking of whip-poorwills, I was waked after midnight by one of those feathered hellions and lay there counting his chants. He got up to one hundred and fifty-eight and then suddenly said, "Whip—" and stopped dead. I like to believe that his mate, at the end of her patience, finally let him have it.

My unfortunate tendency to count "*you* knows" is practically making a female whippoorwill out of me. Listening to a radio commentator, not long ago, discussing the

recent meeting of the United Nations, I thought I was going mad when I heard him using "you know" as a noun, until I realized that he had shortened United Nations Organization to UNO and was pronouncing it, you know, as if it were "*you* know."

A typical example of speech *you*-knowed to death goes like this. "The other day I saw, you know, Harry Johnson, the, you know, former publicity man for, you know, the Charteriss Publishing Company, and, you know, what he wanted to talk about, strangely enough, was, you know, something you'd never guess. . . ."

This curse may have originated simultaneously on Broadway and in Hollywood, where such curses often originate. About twenty-five years ago, or perhaps longer, theatre and movie people jammed their sentences with "you know what I mean?" which was soon shortened to "you *know?*" That had followed the over-use, in the 1920's, of "you see?" or just plain "see?" These blights often disappear finally, but a few have stayed and will continue to stay, such as "Well" and "I mean to say" and "I mean" and "The fact is." Others seem to have mercifully passed out of lingo into limbo, such as, to go back a long way, "Twenty-three, skiddoo" and "So's your old man" and "I don't know nothin' from nothin'" and "Believe you me." About five years ago both men and women were saying things like "He has a new Cadillac job with a built-in bar deal in the back seat" and in 1958 almost everything anybody mentioned, or even wrote about, was "triggered." Arguments were triggered, and allergies, and divorces, and even love affairs. This gun-and-bomb verb seemed to make the jumpiest of the jumpy even jumpier, but it has almost died out now, and I trust that I have not triggered its revival.

It was in Paris, from late 1918 until early 1920, that there was a glut—an American glut, to be sure—of "You said it" and "You can say that again," and an American Marine I knew, from Montana, could not speak any sentence of agreement or concurrence without saying, "It *is*, you *know*." Fortunately, that perhaps original use of "*you know*" did not seem to be imported into America.

I am reluctantly making notes for a possible future volume to be called *A Farewell to Speech* or *The Decline and Fall of the King's English*. I hope and pray that I shall not have to write the book. Maybe everything, or at least the language, will clear up before it is too late. Let's face it, it better had, that's for sure, and I don't mean maybe.

6

Magical Lady

I can still be heard proclaiming on street corners that *My Fair Lady* has restored comedy to a position of dignity in the theatre. "And where is that lofty plane?" a listener may well ask. "And where has comedy been lying doggo, in your arrogant opinion?"

By dignity I mean the high place attained only when the heart and mind are lifted, equally and at once, by the creative union of perception and grace. Sheer skill or talent is not enough, and neither is the excitation of the retina and eardrum. Something must explode deeper inside the beholder, like a silent skyrocket.

This phenomenon doesn't happen often in comedy, or in anything else, but when it does it's a time for putting out flags. The explosive process is a matter of moments, of course, or peaks, but the remembrance of the whole experience takes on and holds the color of the highest peak which, in the instance at hand, is "The rain in Spain stays mainly in the plain." Critics like to call such a moment magic, but it is a word without sweat. Perfection, which achieves its end by labor, is better. The perfect tribute to perfection in comedy is not immediate laughter, but a curious and instantaneous tendency of the eyes to fill.

"The Rain in Spain" is not an interpolated song, but a scene mightily activating the characters and advancing the plot. Music too often blurs the spoken word and the speaking voice, which have certain nuances and subtleties of their own. Some of the rich Negro speech of *Porgy* is lost in a fully orchestrated *Porgy and Bess*. Music has traditionally covered up poor stories, but it should not obscure exceptional ones. Alan Jay Lerner and Frederick Loewe enhance Shaw's *Pygmalion* with occasional music and lyrics, instead of burying it under them. A Shaw play must not be stopped, even by an Ethel Merman or an Ezio Pinza.

Comedy is a serious art, and its high uses on the stage are too often subordinated to song, famous personalities, big production numbers and ballet. Who can ever forget the music and lyrics of *Oklahoma!* or remember any of its comic dialogue? John Jay Chapman once said, "When I put down a book by Stevenson, I swear I am hungry for something to read." How many musical comedies have left adults at the end exhilarated and humming, but hungry for something to think about? The typical musical, presenting the antics of dotty guys with dotless dice and dreamy dolls, gobs and dames, G. I.'s and dames, males and mice, however wonderfully effective, has given us nothing for intelligence to deal with. Comedy has ceased to be a challenge to the mental processes. It has become a therapy of relaxation, a kind of tranquillizing drug.

The fact that a Shaw comedy, described by him as "didactic art" and dealing with a "dry as dust" subject, namely the phonetic dedication of a middle-aged cerebretonic ectomorph to a young female laboratory specimen, seems likely to become the most popular entertainment in Broadway history is a great argument in favor of something more inspiring in the comic theatre than what we have been getting. Furthermore, the trite but tremendous tradition of young love, with its croonings and cooings and its promised consummation in the mindless land of Ever After, has taken a lovely beating. Mr. Lerner and Mr. Loewe have done honorable justice to the peculiar notions of the old Master, one of which was that Eliza, after the play is over, marries Freddy. Shaw's didactics and anti-biological urge are respectfully preserved for listeners with minds as well as hearts.

Shaw plays, suitable for transfiguring, don't grow on trees, but now that we have risen so high with him and his American adapters, there is a tendency to look around for other enhanceable material. Perhaps we have to go back to the period of *Pygmalion*. There Messrs. Lerner and Loewe would find several attractive Henry James items, all of them novels: *Washington Square*, which became *The Heiress* on the stage; *The Sense of the Past*, on which *Berkeley Square* was based, and James's own favorite work, *The Ambassadors.* This last is about a young American in Paris involved with the charming, but older, Countess de Vionnet. A middle-aged American named Strether comes over to break up the romance, with what could hardly be called the invaluable help of a pretty American girl from Massachusetts. Strether is won over to the side of the countess in the end. I can hear him now singing one of the piece's major themes, "If you haven't had your life, what have you had?"

There are many excuses for the decline of comedy in our time. Writers in the Atomic Era and the Aspirin Age are twenty-four centuries more jittery than Aristophanes, and scarcely in a Restoration or even nineteen-twenties mood. The fact that the theatre is officially suspect is the worst hindrance of all to creative humor. A nation in which a Congressman can seriously ask, "Do you believe the artist is a special person?" is a nation living in cultural jeopardy. Better writing is coming out of England, where a writer can work in mental serenity. Enid Bagnold showed us in *The Chalk Garden* the loving care and graceful touch of a playwright who doesn't have to keep looking over her shoulder.

Most of our young comic talents are making their fortunes in television factories. The few who emerge are either what George Axelrod calls "playwrotes"—guys who write one good comedy and are then spoiled by success —or dramatists devoted to what Paddy Chayefsky praises so highly as "naked emotion." I can only pray that clothed sensibility will survive, too, brave in the midst of peril, like an Englishman calmly dressing for dinner on the edge of the jungle.

Meanwhile, we can keep going back to *My Fair Lady*, which is flying with invisible wings at the Mark Hellinger, even if we have to rise at six o'clock and get in line for standing room.

7

Friends, Romans, Countrymen, Lend Me Your Ear Muffs

I have an intimate friend—I shall call him Walter Ego, which is close enough—who may be seen at parties flicking his right ear with his hand, as if to drive away an invisible buzzing bee. This chap is going on sixty-seven, but it is not a ringing in his aging ears that bothers him. What does bother him is the pronunciation of words— crippled or wingless words that escape, all distorted, the careless human lips of our jittery time.

Walter, as you may possibly have guessed, is unable to see, and this has made his ears hypersensitive to sound.

Blindness, to dispose of a myth, does not actually increase the auditory function; it merely sharpens the focus of attention. Mr. Ego has been keeping irritable track, for some years now, of the pronunciations that disturb him most. I shall set some of them down here, in the wistful—nay, the futile—hope that it may do something to restore the art of articulation, the dignity of diction, and thus improve the process of communication, for precision of communication is important, more important than ever, in our era of hair-trigger balances, when a false, or misunderstood, word may create as much disaster as a sudden thoughtless act.

I might begin with the word "futile," which I have already used. Most Americans pronounce it as if it were spelled "fewtle," and this the English listener finds most annoying, for he almost always gives the "ile" its full chord-like value. Actually (to use a word with which the English begin almost every third sentence), there are three permissible pronunciations of "futile." Webster recognizes, in order, "fū'tĭl" and "fū't'l" (which is our old friend "fewtle"). The Oxford English Dictionary prefers "fū'tĭl," but also allows the "ile" to be pronounced as in "smile," and, as I have said, most Englishmen prefer the long "i." Both the smiling "futile" and "fewtle" bother me, for I am a "fū'tĭl" man. Curiously enough, the English, who make such a fuss about our "fewtle," are not at all disconcerted by their own disfiguring of the word "figure," which they invariably pronounce "figga." Nothing, alas, will ever be done about this fewtle figga in the pattern of sound.

The irascible Walter Ego places high in the list of wounded buzzing bees the pronunciation, both here and abroad, of "schedule." He does not so much mind the British "shedule"—that, after all, is a matter of shooling; what offends his ear is the tendency of most Americans to say "skedjuel." Walter has had the audacity to object to the pronunciation of various words by the recent President of the United States who said "skedjl," thus losing the long "u" but avoiding the nonexistent "el." Mr. Eisenhower, who was understandably pressed for time in speech, as he was in all things, except perhaps teeing off, slid over "intellectual" and "gradual," turning them into "intellectchl" and "gradjl."

Mr. Ego, whom I shall hereinafter call I, for he is I, and I am a busy man myself, has been particularly agonized by what has happened verbally to certain present participles in our great, jumpy land. I find that 84.5 per cent of Americans of both sexes stretch into three syllables such words as "sparkling," "struggling," and "battling." The bastard sound of "sparkeling" is heard, day in and night out, in radio and television commercials, and even trained actors are afflicted by these three-syllable enormities. In trying to figure it all out, I began with an impossible assumption—namely, that 84.5 per cent of American men and women were sick in bed on the day when the formation of the present participle from words ending in "le" was taken up in school. We are much too healthy a nation for that. The chief culprit, it now seems to me, is, and always has been, the writer of lyrics for popular songs. Fifty years ago, one of them came up with "We'll be cuddle-in' soon" (by the light of the silvery moon, of course), and only a little later everybody was singing, from "Waiting for the Robert E. Lee," the memorable "Join that shuffle-in' throng." Then the lyricist of "The tumble-in' tumbleweeds," and many others, joined the shuffle-in' throng.

The present decade is one of formlessness in literature, in drama, and in comedy as well as in speech. We know now that the planet is not spherical but pear-shaped, and the shape of the pear has spoiled the perfect dimensions of the circular. Automation has also got its ugly hand into the general disfigurement of shape. Sentences now run themselves, instead of being guided. Thus a certain cigarette "travels and gentles the smoke," and a certain newspaper reads itself (that is, "reads faster and livelier"), and various automobiles handle easily—handle themselves, it must be, so that the preoccupied driver can be left to his own concerns, which consist largely of banging into other cars. This kind of reversal, or inversion, this careless and reckless transition between the transitive and the intransitive, is a threat to meaning and clarity that can't be lightly dismissed. Let's take a brief, frightening glance at what could happen if it becomes a plague rather than a mere nuisance.

If the ramparts we watch begin watching themselves, in our self-service, push-button age, we shall be in imminent peril. I find my gloomy thoughts (my gloomy thoughts find easily nowadays) imagining all kinds of verbal atrocities. "The voyeur confessed that the naked model ogled hungrily." And the spreading affliction must already have infected the cops. "The struggle in the dimly lit basement eyewitnessed fewly, if at all, according to the police."

The Madison Avenue advertising men, the men in the gray-flannel minds, deliberately take advantage of all the slur and sloppiness, because when purists object, it simply serves to spread the news of a product advertised in lousy English. Incidentally, some months ago I offered to sell to a brewery—any brewery—the slogan "We still brew good like we used to could," but for some odd reason I have had no takers. I have been expecting to hear from P. Ballantine. This brewing company's most relentless singing commercial stretches "precisely" and "nicely" into extra syllables to rhyme with "icily." This lingual lignification, or grammatical dystrophy, or whatever the ailment might be called, long ago infected the lovely word "evening," which Webster firmly points out should be pronounced "ēv′nĭng," but who consults Webster for anything except definitions? Certainly not one of my favorite news commentators, who was probably reared in a family that said "ev-en-ing," so that he is now incurable.

The sound I am most conscious of, I think, is the simple sound of "uh," which 69.8 per cent of American women, in talking, combine with the word "and." The record so far, in my circle, was set by a matron who got seventeen "and-uhs" into an account of some household happening. In this kind of suffixing, however, the English, even some of their trained actors, far surpass our women, and it is the English men who are mainly the guilty ones. "Actually, I was in India for three months, but-um-uh that was many years ago." There is, to be sure, a simple "but-uh," which is heard on all sides in London, and from all classes, though mainly the upper class, but-uh the very best but-

44

uh is the but-um-uh. There is one important distinction to be made between the American female's "and-uh" and-uh the English male's "but-um-uh." The American woman puts in the "uh" because she is not quite sure what she is about to say, having got ahead of her story or lost track of it, whereas the "but-um-uh" of the English is used as a gesture, like the waving of a lighted cigarette in the air, the striking of a match, or the lifting of a highball glass.

In that part of the Middle West where I grew up, amidst verbal wonders and linguistic portents, the stultification of English was caused by the decapitation of words as well as by unwonted lengthening. The letter "o" at times seemed to be about to drop out of the spoken language, not only in the perhaps justifiable "possum" for "opossum" (no worse than Shakespeare's "pard" for "leopard") but also in "official," which became "fishel," and "obituary," which became "bituary." Now and then the letter "a" was removed from one word and affixed to another, as in "She got pendicitis and then aperitonitis." Some of my mother's folks pronounced "laugh" as if it were spelled "la-yuff." In a few of the older ladies of the family it still persists, and one of them, when I was in Columbus last, wonderfully made five syllables out of "laughingly"—"la-yuff-ing-i-ly." I wouldn't have her change it for the world.

Sometimes it seems to me, in listening to radio's singing commercials, that both sponsors and advertising agencies are giving up the struggle to communicate, washing their hands of sense and meaning. The sales singing is now often turned over to tiny tots. One of the commercials is charmingly sung in unison by two little girls who can't be older than five. My trained ear, my trained and sprained ear, has listened to their duet a dozen times, trying to make out what in the name of heaven they are singing. Fortunately, a male adult voice comes in at the end, spells out the name of the product, then repeats it, and tells what it is for. This man claims that the small maidens with the piping voices are advertising "T-H-R-I-V-O—Thrivo dog food." He ought to know what he is talking about, and what they are singing about, but I can't get it out of my head that he is just guessing.

The trouble is not with my radio, which listens fine, and travels and limpids the sound. The trouble is it just doesn't speak any known language. The other day, it said, "Wall Street stocks firmed today all along the line." Maybe I should see a psychiatrist, or hear one, but they are all so busy that I know of none who consults easily. Besides, my head will not examine willingly, for the simple reason that I am afraid of being put away. This doesn't make sense, either, because then I would get away from what I am trying to get away from. I guess I have just gone curazy, turying to make sense out of the sound and the fury, or, rather, the unsound and the fuzzy.

Nowadays, when practically every prisoner, it sometimes seems to me, is escaping from durance vile, or has escaped, or is planning escape, the annoying word "escapee" is heard over the air almost continually. I don't often disagree with Webster, but I do disagree with his definition of "escapee." According to Webster, an escapist is one who seeks escape, an escaper is one in the act of escaping, and an escapee is one who has escaped. To me, the escapees are the prison guards whom the escapers have escaped, just as employees are those employed by employers. But let us not end by brooding on this mishmash of hairsplitting. Let us, instead, end on a sentence or two recently spoken by an elderly woman in my Connecticut community. The other day, she said, "I'll just nice this room up before the people get here." I happen to like this woman and the way she says things, if only because they are a constant challenge to my powers of comprehension (to her, "Bavarian" is always "Baravian"). She once said to me, "Who do you doctor with in New York?" I didn't know whether she wanted to know whom I general practice with or specialize with, or whether she meant medicalwise, surgicalwise, or ophthalmologicalwise.

A living language is an expanding language, to be sure, but care should take itself that the language does not crack like a dry stick in the process, leaving us all miserably muddling in a monstrous miasma of mindless and meaningless mumbling. The other morning, just as the birds that brighten my place in Connecticut were ushering in the day with song, a woman came chattering into my dreams, saying, "We can sleep twenty people in this house in a pinch, but we can only eat twelve." I woke up with a start and a mumble. Outside my window, to my comfort, a catbird and a wren were making sweet sense.

8

The Last Clock

A FABLE FOR THE TIME, SUCH AS IT IS, OF MAN

In a country the other side of tomorrow, an ogre who had eaten a clock and had fallen into the habit of eating clocks was eating a clock in the clockroom of his castle when his ogress and their ilk knocked down the locked door and shook their hairy heads at him.

"Wulsa malla?" gurgled the ogre, for too much clock oil had turned all his "t"s to "l"s.

"Just look at this room!" exclaimed the ogress, and they all looked at the room, the ogre with eyes as fogged as the headlights of an ancient limousine. The stone floor of the room was littered with fragments of dials, oily coils and springs, broken clock hands, and pieces of pendulums. "I've brought a doctor to look at you," the ogress said.

The doctor wore a black beard, carried a black bag, and

gave the ogre a black look. "This case is clearly not in my area," he said.

The ogre struck three, and the doctor flushed.

"This is a case for a clockman," the doctor said, "for the problem is not what clocks have done to the ogre but what the ogre has done to clocks."

"Wulsa malla?" the ogre gurgled again.

"Eating clocks has turned all his 't's to 'l's," the ogress said. "That's what clocks have done to him."

"Then your clockman may have to call in consultation a semanticist or a dictionist or an etymologist or a syntax-man," the non-clock doctor said, and he bowed stiffly and left the room.

The next morning, the ogress brought into the clock-room a beardless man with a box of tools under his arm. "I've brought a clockman to see you," she told the ogre.

"No, no, no," said the beardless man with the box of tools. "I'm not a clockman. I thought you said clogman. I'm a clogman. I cannot ethically depart from my area, which is clogged drains and gutters. I get mice out of pipes, and bugs out of tubes, and moles out of tiles, and there my area ends." The clogman bowed and went away.

"Wuld wuzzle?" the ogre wanted to know. He hic-cuped, and something went *spong!*

"That was an area man, but the wrong area," the ogress explained. "I'll get a general practitioner." And she went away and came back with a general practitioner.

"This is a waste of time," he said. "As a general prac-titioner, modern style, I treat only generals. This patient is not even a private. He sounds to me like a public place

—a clock tower, perhaps, or a belfry."

"What should I do?" asked the ogress. "Send for a tower man, or a belfry man?"

"I shall not venture an opinion," the general practitioner said. "I am a specialist in generals, one of whom has just lost command of his army and of all his faculties, and doesn't know what time it is. Good day." And the general practitioner went away.

The ogre cracked a small clock, as if it were a large walnut, and began eating it. "Wulsy wul?" the ogre asked.

The ogress, who could now talk clocktalk fluently, even oilily, but wouldn't, left the room to look up specialists in an enormous volume entitled *Who's Who in Areas*. She soon became lost in a list of titles: clockmaker, clock-smith, clockwright, clockmonger, clockician, clockome-trist, clockologist, and a hundred others dealing with clockness, clockism, clockship, clockdom, clockation, clockition, and clockhood.

The ogress decided to call on an old inspirationalist who had once advised her father not to worry about a giant he was worrying about. The inspirationalist had said to the ogress's father, "Don't pay any attention to it, and it will go away." And the ogress's father had paid no atten-tion to it, and it had gone away, taking him with it, and this had pleased the ogress. The inspirationalist was now a very old man whose inspirationalism had become a jum-ble of mumble. "The final experience should not be mum-mum," he mumbled.

The ogress said, "But what is mummum?"

"Mummum," said the inspirationalist, "is what the final

50

experience should not be." And he mumbled to a couch, lay down upon it, and fell asleep.

As the days went on, the ogre ate all the clocks in the town—mantel clocks, grandfather clocks, traveling clocks, stationary clocks, alarm clocks, eight-day clocks, steeple clocks, and tower clocks—sprinkling them with watches, as if the watches were salt and pepper, until there were no more watches. People overslept, and failed to go to work, or to church, or anyplace else where they had to be on time. Factories closed down, shopkeepers shut up their shops, schools did not open, trains no longer ran, and people stayed at home. The town council held an emergency meeting and its members arrived at all hours, and some did not show up at all.

A psychronologist was called to the witness stand to testify as to what should be done. "This would appear to be a clear case of clock-eating, but we should not jump so easily to conclusions," he said. "We have no scientific data whatever on clock-eating, and hence no controlled observation. All things, as we know, are impossible in this most impossible of all impossible worlds. That being the case, no such thing as we think has happened could have happened. Thus the situation does not fall within the frame of my discipline. Good day, gentlemen." The psychronologist glanced at where his wristwatch should have been and, not finding it there, was disturbed. "I have less than no time at all," he said, "which means that I am late for my next appointment." And he hurriedly left the council room.

The Lord Mayor of the town, arriving late to preside

over the council meeting, called a clockonomist to the stand. "What we have here," said the clockonomist, "appears on the surface to be a clockonomic crisis. It is the direct opposite of what is known, in my field, as a glut of clocks. That is, instead of there being more clocks than the consumer needs, so that the price of clocks would decrease, the consumer has consumed all the clocks. This should send up the price of clocks sharply, but we are faced with the unique fact that there are no clocks. Now, as a clockonomist, my concern is the economy of clocks, but where there are no clocks there can be no such economy. The area, in short, has disappeared."

"What do you suggest, then?" demanded the Lord Mayor.

"I suggest," said the clockonomist, "that it is now high time I go into some other line of endeavor, or transfer my clockonomy to a town which has clocks. Good day, gentlemen." And the clockonomist left the council room.

A clockosopher next took the witness chair. "If it is high time," he said, "then there is still time. The question is this: How high is high time? It means, if it means anything, which I doubt, that it is time to act. I am not an actor, gentlemen, but a clockosopher, whose osophy is based upon clocks, not necessarily upon their physical existence, but upon clocks as a concept. We still have clocks as a concept, but this meeting is concerned solely with clocks as objects. Thus its deliberations fall well outside my range of interests, and I am simply wasting time here, or would be if there were time to waste. Good day, gentlemen." And the clockosopher left the council room.

The clockmakers of the town, who had been subpoenaed, were then enjoined, in a body, from making more clocks. "You have been supplying the ogre with clocks," the Lord Mayor said severely, "whether intentionally or willy-nilly is irrelevant. You have been working hand in glove, or clock in hand, with the ogre." The clockmakers left, to look for other work.

"I should like to solve this case by deporting the ogre," the Lord Mayor said, "but, as a container of clocks, he would have to be exported, not deported. Unfortunately, the law is clear on this point: Clocks may not be exported in any save regulation containers, and the human body falls outside that legal definition."

Three weeks to the day after the ogre had eaten the last clock, he fell ill and took to his bed, and the ogress sent for the chief diagnostician of the Medical Academy, a diagnostician familiar with so many areas that totality itself had become to him only a part of wholeness. "The trouble is," said the chief diagnostician, "we don't know what the trouble is. Nobody has ever eaten all the clocks before, so it is impossible to tell whether the patient has clockitis, clockosis, clockoma, or clocktheria. We are also faced with the possibility that there may be no such diseases. The patient may have one of the minor clock ailments, if there are any, such as clockets, clockles, clocking cough, ticking pox, or clumps. We shall have to develop area men who will find out about such areas, if such areas exist, which, until we find out that they do, we must assume do not."

"What if he dies?" demanded the ogress eagerly.

"Then," said the chief diagnostician, "we shall bury him." And the chief diagnostician left the ogre's room and the castle.

The case of the town's clocklessness was carried to the Supreme Council, presided over by the Supreme Magistrate. "Who is prosecuting whom?" the Supreme Magistrate demanded.

The Supreme Prosecutor stood up. "Let somebody say something, and I will object," he said. "We have to start somewhere, even if we start nowhere."

A housewife took the witness stand. "Without a clock," she said, "I cannot even boil a three-minute egg."

"Objection," said the Supreme Prosecutor. "One does not *have* to boil a three-minute egg. A three-minute egg, by definition, has already been boiled for three minutes, or it wouldn't be a three-minute egg."

"Objection sustained," droned the Supreme Magistrate.

The Leader of the Opposition then took the stand. "The party in power has caused the mess in the ogre's castle," he said.

"Objection," said the Supreme Prosecutor. "There isn't any party in power. The ogre was the party in power, but he no longer has any power. Furthermore, the mess caused by the party cleaning up the mess caused by the party in power, which is no longer in power, would be worse than the mess left by the party that was in power."

"Objection sustained," droned the Supreme Magistrate.

The Secretary of Status Quo was the next man to take the stand. "We are not getting anywhere," he said, "and therefore we should call a summit conference without agenda. A summit conference without agenda is destined to get even less than nowhere, but its deliberations will impress those who are impressed by deliberations that get less than nowhere. This has unworked in the past, and it will unwork now. If we get less than nowhere fast enough, we shall more than hold our own, for everything is circular and cyclical, and where there are no clocks, clockwise and counterclockwise are the same."

"Objection," said the Supreme Prosecutor. "We are dealing here with a purely internal matter, caused by the consumer's having consumed all the clocks."

"Objection sustained," droned the Supreme Magistrate.

The Man in the Street now took the stand. "Why don't we use sundials?" he demanded.

"I challenge the existence of the witness," said the Supreme Prosecutor. "He says he is the Man in the Street, but he is, in fact, the Man in the Supreme Council Room. Furthermore, sundials work only when the sun is shining, and nobody cares what time it is when the sun is shining."

The Man in the Street left the witness chair, and nobody noticed his going, since the Supreme Prosecutor had established the fact that he had not been there.

There was a long silence in the Supreme Council Room, a silence so deep one could have heard a pin drop, if a pin had been dropped, but nobody dropped a pin. What everybody in the Council Room heard, in the long, deep silence, was the slow tick-tock of a clock, a wall clock, the clock on the wall behind the Supreme Magistrate's bench. The officials and the witnesses and the spectators had grown so used to not hearing clocks it wasn't until the clock struck the hour that they realized there was a wall clock on the wall.

The Supreme Magistrate was the first to speak. "Unless I am mightily mistaken, and I usually am, we have here the solution to all our problems," he said, "namely, a clock. Unless there is an objection and I sustain the objection, which I do not think I shall, we will place this clock in the clock tower of the town, where it can be seen by one and all. Then we shall once again know what time it is. The situation will be cleared up, and the case dismissed."

"One minute," said the Supreme Prosecutor, and everybody waited a minute until he spoke again. "What is to prevent the ogre from eating the clock in the clock tower?"

"If you are asking me," said the Supreme Magistrate, "I do not know, but I do not have to confess my ignorance, since affirmations of this sort do not fall within my jurisdiction."

A bailiff stepped to the bench and handed the Supreme Magistrate a folded note. The Magistrate glanced at it, took off his glasses, and addressed all those present. "The ogre is dead," he announced.

"Objection," said the Supreme Prosecutor.

"Objection overruled," said the Magistrate, "if you are objecting to the fact of the ogre's death."

"I accept the ogre's death as a fact," said the Prosecutor, "but we are moving too fast, and I should like to call a specialist to the stand." And he called a specialist to the stand.

"I am a collector," said the specialist. "The clock on the wall is the only clock there is. This makes it not, in fact, a clock but a collector's item, or museum piece. As such, it must be placed in the town museum. One does not spend the coins in a museum. The wineglasses in a museum do not hold wine. The suits of armor in a museum do not contain knights. The clocks in a museum do not tell time. This clock, the last clock there is, must therefore be allowed to run down, and then placed in the museum, with proper ceremonies, addresses, and the like."

"I move that this be done," the Prosecutor said.

"I should like to continue to know, as much as everybody else, what time it is," pronounced the Supreme Magistrate. "Under the circumstances, however, there is but one thing I can do in conformity with the rule which establishes the inalienable fact that the last clock is a collector's item, or museum piece. I therefore decree that the last clock, the clock here on the wall, be allowed to run down, and then placed in the town museum, with proper ceremonies, addresses, and the like."

The next day, at nine minutes of twelve o'clock noon, the last clock ran down and stopped. It was then placed in the town museum, as a collector's item, or museum piece, with proper ceremonies, addresses, and the like. Among those who spoke were the Lord Mayor, the Secretary of Status Quo, and the Supreme Magistrate. They all chose the same subjects, without verbs or predicates, and the subjects were these: glorious past, unlimited opportunity, challenging future, dedication, inspired leadership, enlightened followership, rededication, moral fibre, spiritual values, outer space, inner man, higher ideals, lower taxes, unflagging enthusiasm, unswerving devotion, co-ordinated efforts, dedicated rededication, and rededicated dedication.

After that, nobody in the town ever knew what time it was. Factories and schools remained closed, church bells no longer rang, because the bell ringers no longer knew when to ring them, dates and engagements were no longer made, because nobody knew when to keep them. Trains no longer ran, so nobody left town and no strangers arrived in town to tell the people what time it was. Eventually, the sands of a nearby desert moved slowly and inexorably toward the timeless town, and in the end it was buried.

Eras, epochs, and aeons passed before a party of explorers from another planet began digging in the sands above the buried town. They were descendants of people from Earth who had reached Venus a thousand years before and intermarried with Venusians. Among them were a young man and a young woman, and it was their fortune to be the first to come upon the ancient library of the old inspirationalist. Among some papers still preserved upon his desk were the last things he had written— bits of poetry from the grand Old Masters and the minor poets. One of these fragments read, "How goes the night, boy? The moomoon is down. I have not heard the clock." And the very last words his wavery pen had put on paper:

> We can make our lives sublime,
> And, departing, leave behind us,
> Mummum in the sands of time.

"What is mummum?" the young woman asked.

58

"I don't know," the young man said, "but something tells me we shall find a lot of it." They went on digging, and, in the end, came upon the last clock in the town museum, so clogged with sand they could not tell what it had once been used for, and so they marked it "Antique mechanism. Function uncertain. Possibly known to the ancients as mummmum." And they took it back to Venus, in a cargo rocket ship, with other mysterious relics of the Time of Man on Earth.

9

Such a Phrase as Drifts Through Dreams

Something central and essential in the mechanism of meaning began losing its symmetry last summer. It was as if the maiden spring of sense had suddenly become matron-sprung. At first I thought the fault must be in myself, some flaw of comprehension or concentration, aggravated by the march of time. Then I realized one June afternoon at a cocktail party in Bermuda that the trouble was largely female, or at least seemed to originate in that sex, like so many other alarming things.

At this party, a woman from the Middle West began telling me about some legal involvement her daughter and son-in-law had got into. I didn't have the vaguest idea what it was all about, and was merely feigning attention, when she ended her cloudy recital on a note of triumph. "So finally they decided to leave it where sleeping dogs lie," she said. I was upon it in a moment, hastily assuming my best Henry James garden-party manner. "How perfectly charming of them both, dear lady," I wonderfully cried. "One can only hope the barristers for the other side will tumble for it, hook, line, and barrel. To be sure, they may overtake it in their stride, in which case may the devil pay the hindmost." Upon this my companion cautiously withdrew to the safer company of younger minds.

The charmingly tainted idiom of the lady of the sleeping dogs must have infected other members of her circle in Somerset, among them a beautiful young woman from Geneva, New York, who told me, in another Bermuda landscape with figures, "We are not going to hide our heads in the sand like kangaroos." This was just what my harassed understanding and tortured spirits needed. I was, it is not too much to say, saved by the twisted and inspired simile, and whenever I think I hear the men coming with the stretcher or the subpoena, I remember those kangaroos with their heads in the sand, and I am ready to face anything again.

The kangaroo, it has always seemed to me, is Exhibit A among the evidence supporting the contention of some of us that Nature has a grotesque and lovely sense of humor. I think the Geneva lady's kangaroos would be far more effective head-hiders than ostriches. Any creature coming upon a kangaroo upright would not be frightened by its comic head and little forelegs, but a sudden view of its strange and enormous rear quarters, protruding from the earth, would surely be enough to give pause to a prowling tiger or a charging rhino. (Quibblers who have pounced upon the fact that there are no tigers or rhinos in Australia should remember that these kangaroos are Bermuda kangaroos.) I was not the first to think of the head-hiding kangaroos of Bermuda, alas, but I shall be the last to forget them.

It was only a fortnight later that a counterpart of the Bermuda ladies, this one the proud mother of a young man who had just completed his first year as a history teacher, sat down beside me at an indoor cocktail party in New York and leaped into a discussion of history professors in general. "It is not easy to make them colleagues," she said. "They are always looking down each other's noses."

I let my awareness deal with this troubled idiom for a long Jamesian moment before replying. "At least," I said, with an old-world smile, "when there is so much smoke one knows one is in Denmark. But be of good cheer. I can fairly see the butter melting in their mouths now." My companion was delightfully equal to it. "Oh, but I am sure that he will," she said.

The summer malady of incoherence soon spread, as I was afraid it would, to printers and proofreaders, or, at any rate, to one or two saddled with the admittedly onerous task of helping to get some stories of mine into book form. Ours is a precarious language, as every writer knows, in which the merest shadow line often separates

affirmation from negation, sense from nonsense, and one sex from the other. Forty years ago, *The Candle,* a literary monthly published at Ohio State University, ruined the point of a mild little essay of mine by garbling a salient quotation so that it came out "The gates of hell shall now prevail."

One linotyper I have never met became co-author of a piece of mine last year by introducing a bear into the story. He simply made one out of a bead that was lying around in the middle of the narrative. This set me to brooding, and for weeks I lay awake at night, in my fashion, playing unhappily with imaginary havoc wrought by single letter changes in the printed word. I still remember a few of them: "A stitch in time saves none . . . There's no business like shoe business . . . Lafayette, we ate here . . . Don, give up the ship."

Lucidity in Bermuda (we are now back in Bermuda)

is further complicated by the special idiom of the Negro population, so that turning from a lady at a lawn party to a cook or maid in a cottage or guest house is, you might say, to jump out of the frying pan into the deep blue sea. "They had an upside-down wedding," for example, does not mean that the participants stood on their heads, but only that a child had been born to the contracting couple before the ceremony. "I hoped," one Negro lady said to me, "that my sister would be married before the baby came, but God had other plans for her." Here the meaning is clear enough and only the morality is blurred, as in the now celebrated case of the Bermudian wife who, in seeking a divorce, insisted to the worshipful magistrate that her grounds were simple and sufficient: "I have reason to believe that my husband is not the father of my last child."

In Martha's Vineyard last August—is there something about islands that fogs the clarity of speech?—I fell into conversation with an actress I had known in my Greenwich Village, or devil-may-care days, and we began counting our Village friends of thirty years ago, separating the dead from the crazy, and both from those who had moved to Hollywood, or at least uptown. It turned out that Gloria Mundy, as I shall call her, was still living in the same old place on Christopher Street, or Commerce, or Wherever. "Her apartment was broken into so often this year, she finally had to have it burglarized," my old friend told me.

My aging mind had to turn that over several times before I could find anything to say. "You mean there's a *company* that burglarizes apartments now?" I finally demanded. "What do you do—call them up and tell them when you won't be home?"

My companion eyed me warily. "You don't have to not be home," she said.

"Most people are not home when their apartments are burglarized," I told her. "It's like foolproofing a part in a play. The author would rather not have anybody around. Are you sure Gloria didn't have the place just alarmed?"

"I don't know what you're talking about," said my old friend quietly, moving a foot or so farther away.

"It's much simpler and a lot cheaper to install a burglar alarm than to have your apartment completely burglarized," I told her.

"I hate writers," she said, after a long pause. "They're such Puritans about everything. You can't even use a figure of speech the wrong way."

"We are a brave lot, though," I insisted. "We stand at Armageddon and we battle for the word while the very Oedipus of reason crumbles beneath us."

"Let's go to the Harborside and have a drink," she said, and we went there and had a long, cold drink, in silence. That is the best way to commune with an actress.

I am back at my home in Connecticut now, resting up after a bad year among the meaning-manglers, the lunatype machines, and the typowriters. The worst that has happened in the realm of the anti-perspicuous was a letter I got whose third sentence began like this: "Even whether you haven't been there or not yet . . ." I just threw it away. To be sure, radio and television go on speaking

their special kind of broken English, but it is rather comforting after a long day of trying to write simple declarative English sentences. "It is possible that the killer is probably in the house now," said a man on one of TV's half-hour mysteries. It gave me a moral for a future fable, which I jotted down and filed: "A pinch of probably is worth a pound of perhaps." Then there was the moment in a Sherlock Holmes television program when Doctor Watson stoutly defended (or tried to, anyway) the innocence of a guilty woman. "Mrs. *Burchard?* She couldn't be less harmless!"

Our community in the lovely foothills of the Berkshires wears a special radiance the year round in the person of a French lady whom I shall call Renée. The accuracy of her English and the quality of her clarity depend on the weather in her heart, which changes with the caprice of island winds. In an hour of impatience she once said to the local telephone operator, "What is the name of the Macleans?" The operator, who loves and understands Renée, like everybody else, did not say, "The Macleans," but simply, "Orchard 2-6338."

Renée is mistress of what I call not the dangling participle, but the dazzling participle, often, when excited, using it in place of the past tense. "How did you like the concert at Tanglewood last night?" I asked her one day.

"I was fascinating," she said.

Renée is always fascinating, but never more so than on two unforgettable occasions. One of these was the evening she told a little circle of her admirers about a visit she had made years ago to Andalusia. "I am with this airedale in Spain," was the way she began her recital, and I shall never forget it. She is a social critic, too, and I am a fond collector of some of her rare pronouncements, of which my favorite is this: "The womans are stronger at the bottom." He who denies that simple statement of truth will receive my glove across his cheek.

Some fifteen years ago, our usually tranquil community was violently upset by the attempted murder of a woman. The State Police questioned us all, and did not come off very well with either Renée or me. "What kind of an artist are you?" a detective asked me, and I must have looked guilty as hell. I finally said, "I refuse to answer that question on the ground that it might incriminate me."

The detective had even tougher sledding with Renée. "One thing I am certain of," he said to her. "Somebody in this town is guilty."

"So am I," said the innocent and wonderful Renée.

The cop stared at her for a long time without a word and then asked, "Where do you live?"

Renée, who was standing on her front porch at the time, waved a hand at her house and said, "I am leeving here." The harassed police officer gave her another long and rueful look, sighed, and said, "So am I," and he went away.

I must go now and feed those Bermuda kangaroos, if I can get their heads out of the sand.

10

A Moment with Mandy

"Why didn't God make bats butterflies?" Mandy suddenly asked me one day. Her questions always demand a grave consideration which her impatience with the slow processes of the adult mind will not tolerate. Mandy is eight, but I state her age with reservations because she is sometimes fourteen or older, and sometimes four or younger. "I want to hang by my heels like a bat," Mandy said, "but I want to be a butterfly. Daddy couldn't spank me then because I would be on the ceiling."

"He could get a stepladder," I said finally.

"I would push it over," she said. "Bang!"

"He could call the fire department, of course," I suggested.

"I would push that over, too," Mandy said, adding, "bang, bang!"

"Butterflies don't hang by their heels," I told her, but she was off on another tack.

"God didn't have to give turtles shells," she told me.

Here I thought I had her, but she does not corner easily in debate. "Turtles are very slow," I explained, "and so God gave them shells they could hide in, to protect themselves from their enemies."

"He could make them faster," Mandy said. "Why didn't he make them faster?" She had me there. I realized, for the first time, that if God had made porcupines and skunks faster, they wouldn't need their quills and vitriol, respectively.

"Why didn't God give us wings?" was her next question, and I began to lecture on that point.

"We have developed wings," I told her, but she cut me off with that topic sentence.

"It took God a million billion years to give us wings," she said. "They are no good." To this she added after a moment's thought, or half a moment's, "We don't have anything."

"We have better sight than dogs. People can see better than they can," I told her.

"Dogs don't bump into things. People bump into things," she said.

"Dogs are guided by better hearing and a better sense of smell than we have," I explained.

"They can't see a light way way off," was her answer to that.

"No, but when the man with the light gets nearer, they can hear him, and then they can smell him," I told her.

She left me flat-footed with a quick passing shot. *"This* light doesn't get nearer, 'cause it's in a lighthouse."

That annoyed me, for I am a bad loser. "All right, all right, then," I snapped. "We'll move the dog nearer the lighthouse. Aren't you going to allow me to score a single point in this colloquy?"

Mandy has a standard answer for any questions she doesn't understand. "No," she said. "Why didn't God give dogs glasses?"

For days I had been practicing some questions of my own for Mandy, and I served them all at once. "Why don't foxes wear foxgloves? Why don't cows wear cowslips? What was it Katy did? If cowboys round up cows, why don't bulldogs round up bulls?"

"Katy who?" Mandy asked, her quick feminine instinct

for scandal making her ignore all the other questions.

"You're too young to know who she was and what she did, and I'm too old to care," I said.

"My daddy says the bugs are going to get everybody." Mandy repeated this prophetic piece of eschatology indifferently, as if it didn't matter.

"Your father was referring to a recent announcement by some scientists that insects are increasing alarmingly on this planet," I told her. "It is my opinion that they are increasing because they are alarmed by the steady increase of human beings."

"I want a swan to get *me*," Mandy said. "What do you want to get *you?*"

I had to give this some thought. "Bear with me," I said. "It isn't easy to decide. It would be colorful and exotic to be got by a green mamba in the Taj Mahal, but my friends would say I was just showing off, and such an ending would also be out of character. I shall probably stumble over my grandson's toy train and break my neck."

Mandy, true to form, lobbed her next question over my head. "What bear?" she said.

"I didn't say anything about a bear," I said.

"You said there was a bear with you," she said, "but there isn't any."

I went back over what I had said and found the bear, but ignored it. "We are getting nowhere faster than usual," I told her.

"What animal would you rather be?" was her next question. I must have been unconsciously preparing for this one.

"I have been a lot of animals," I told her, "but there

72

are also a lot I haven't been. I was never a road hog or a snake in the grass, but I was once a news hound."

"Once my daddy brought an Elk home to our house for dinner," she said, "but he was just a man." She sighed, with the dark light of an old disenchantment in her eyes.

"Men hate to be called animals, but then they form lodges and luncheon clubs and call themselves animals— Elks, Moose, Eagles, Lions, and so on." I was all set to go further with this line of attack or defense, but her interest, after her fashion, had wandered back. "Why don't you want to be a road hog?" she demanded.

"Because they turn turtle, and then the bulls ride up on motorcycles and arrest them."

"Make up a nursery rhyme," Mandy commanded me.

I pretended to be having a hard time making up a nursery rhyme, but my anguish was rigged, for I had made one up long ago for just such an emergency, and I recited it:

"Half a mile from Haverstraw there lived a halfwit fellow,
     Half his house was brick and red, and half was wood
          and yellow;
     Half the town knew half his name but only half could
          spell it.
     If you will sit for half an hour, I've half a mind to
          tell it."

"My daddy makes up nursery rhymes, too," Mandy said. I felt sure her daddy's doggerel would top mine, and it did. "Tell me one of them," I said, and she did.

"Hi diddle diddle, the cat and the fiddle,
     Moscow jumped over the moon."

"That isn't a nursery rhyme," I told her. "That is political science."

"No it isn't," Mandy said.

"Yes it is," I said.

"No it isn't," she said.

"Yes it is," I said.

"No it isn't," she said.

It was at this point, or, to be exact, sword's point, that Mandy's mother and my wife (they are not the same person) entered the room and broke into the debate. "You mustn't say it is if Mr. Thurber says it isn't," her mother told her.

"Are you two arguing again?" my wife wanted to know.

"No," I told her. "I was just explaining to Mandy that she shouldn't get her hopes up if she asks a bull on a motorcycle the way to the next town, and he says, 'Bear left at the church.' There won't be any bear there."

"Yes, there will," Mandy said.

"No, there won't," I said.

"Stop it," my wife said. "It's time to go." We broke it up, but, at the door, I said to Mandy, "Next time I'll explain why the wolf is at the door. It's on account of the stork."

"There isn't any stork, if you mean babies," Mandy said. I am sure she would have explained what she meant, in simple, childish dialectic, but my wife doesn't want me to know the facts of life. "For heaven's sake come on!" she said, and roughly but mercifully dragged me out of there.

MORAL: *If it's words that you would bandy, never tangle with a Mandy.*

11

The Tyranny
of Trivia

An intrepid young literary explorer named Otto Friedrich recently stumbled upon the body of my work lying
sprawled and unburied on the plain, and was distressed
to discover that it had been ravaged by trivia. Mr.
Friedrich thinks that preoccupation with trivia is unbecoming in a writer who belongs to the Solemn if not, indeed, the Sombre tradition of American letters. (How do
you like it now, gentlemen?) The critic, whose findings
appeared in a periodical called *Discovery*, detected what
he called my need to write trivia, and shrewdly coupled
it with "a constant need to make money." By trivia, the
author meant the minor and the unimportant (unless I
misread him, he included sex in this category), and not
grammar, logic, and rhetoric, the big trivia of the dictionary definitions of the word.

I could begin by insisting that Mr. Friedrich has confused my armor with its chink, but this might lead to an intricate and turgid flow of metaphor. It is simpler to say, in another figure, that Trivia Mundi has always been as dear and as necessary to me as her bigger and more glamorous sister, Gloria. They have both long and amicably inhabited a phrase of Coleridge's, "All things both great and small," and I like to think of them taking turns at shooting albatrosses and playing the bassoon.

Some notable trivia, such as the last straw, the lost horseshoe nail, and a piece of string, became involved with larger issues, but my own, I am afraid, never rise to such heights. They consist mainly of a preoccupation, compulsive perhaps, but not obsessive, with words and the alphabet, and most of them never get into print. Their purpose is the side-tracking of worrisome trains of thought. The modern mind has many shuttles and shuntings, the principal one being, I suppose, the reading of mystery novels in bed, to shut out the terrors of the night and the world. Profound thought or plain positive thinking does not conduce to repose. Every man, laying his book aside, still has the night and the world to bypass. The late Bert Leston Taylor used to find comfort in contemplating Canopus, "a star that has no parallax to speak of." I happen to get cold up there in the immeasurable spaces of the outer constellations, and my own system of mental sedation is more mundane.

Some may ward off insomnia by reciting poetry to themselves, such as Tennyson's "The moan of doves in immemorial elms, and murmuring of innumerable bees."

But this has never worked for me, because I invariably begin to take the lines of a poem apart. A friend of mine, fighting off the bells of Poe and avoiding the thickets of Eliot, manages to doze off after several repetitions of, to set it down in a long ramble, "In Xanadu did Kubla Khan a stately pleasure dome decree, where Alph the sacred river ran through caverns measureless to man down to a sunless sea." I tried that several times, discovered the solitary long O in "dome," the six consecutive words containing R, and the last seven R-less words. The dome seemed to stick up a mile above the sunless sea, the rolling Rs trickled away, and I was left stranded in a desiccation of ". . . to man down to a sunless sea."

A mariner so easily marooned in a wasteland of verse finds himself turning away from, say, the lines of Shakespeare that end ". . . how like a god" and toward the old Ed Wynn gag that begins "How would you like to die?" If you don't happen to remember it, a group of murderous gangsters, armed with everything lethal, from a hangman's rope to an enormous bottle of poison, propounded the question to the great comedian. "In Gloria Swanson's arms" was Mr. Wynn's prompt and wistful reply.

I was laughing about that ancient routine a few years ago while lying in a hospital bed, and my alarmed nurse asked me what was the matter. My solitary laughter has always alarmed my nurses, of whom I have had more than twenty since the silent artillery of time began firing at me. I told this particular nurse what I was laughing about, and she thought it over solemnly for a moment. "Well," she said finally, "to me she is every bit as attractive now as she was when I first saw her in a silent film about the French Foreign Legion." She pronounced the last word as if it were "lesion." And here I am again, in the midst of verbal trivia. Nurses' verbal trivia, however, are the very best trivia, and rank high in my collection. I remember a Canadian nurse who read aloud to me from some book or other ". . . that first fine careless rupture," and another who shook me for several long moments one day in 1940 when, in reading aloud from the "Books" department of an erudite journal, she paused to remark that there were notices of eight books about Mussolini. She had come upon, it turned out, a list of short reviews headed "Miscellany." Nurses are wonderful woman and dedicated ministering angels, and they have no time to fritter away on the trivia of spelling and pronunciation.

When a patient is lying at right angles to his nurses and doctors and visitors, and considerably lower—in more ways than one—than all of them, he is in the standard posture for the onset of trivia. I have no doubt that many a dark, serious book has been conceived on a bed, but surely few of them will outlast the wonderful description of wallpaper that was born in the mind of Reginald Gardiner when he lay parallel to the floor and at right angles to everybody. The temper of the supine patient, particularly the postoperative, is capricious and unpredictable, and forms one of the best arguments for the theory and practice of minimum bed rest. My own habit, in bed at home or in the hospital, of exploring words and the alphabet acts to prevent my talking back to the wallpaper, a practice that, except in the case of the upright figure, may be more alarming than amusing.

Most of my hospitalizations were during the war years, when nurses were on twelve-hour shifts—a long time to spend alone with me, especially at night. Many nurses go on the night shift because it is supposed to be easier, but at least one of mine later asked to be transferred to day duty. Nurses, because of their tight and highly specialized vocabulary, are not very good at word games. When I told one apprehensive nurse, around midnight, that only seven capital letters are wholly or partially enclosed—A, B, D, O, P, Q, and R—she promptly printed the entire alphabet on a sheet of paper and told me that H, K, M, N, W, and X are also partially enclosed. She had, you see, set them down squarely on the lines of a sheet of ruled paper. Nurses live by rule and line, and they cannot think of anything as hanging in the circumambient mental air. Occasionally, when I hung a concept there for one of them, she would tiptoe from the room and bring in the night resident doctor. "This patient," as I used to be called with a trace of irritation, was set down as atypical, without significance or syndrome.

One night I asked my nurse if she could think of a seven-letter word in which the letter U appears three times. She sighed and said, "It's probably unusual." I told her that it was and it wasn't, and she slipped out of the room, and a short time later Dr. Conway came in. My doctors always approach my bedside with an air of bluff insincerity, sometimes humming a tune nervously, in an unsuccessful effort to imitate casualness. I asked Dr. Conway if he could find the other six-letter word in suture. "It's right up your alley, but then again it certainly isn't," I told him. An hour later he came back to say that he couldn't find it, and I had to spell it out for him.

Before many days I had Dr. Conway lying awake trying to find a word in which all five vowels appear in order. Even when I told him that three of the vowels come in direct sequence he couldn't get it. Among such words, to release your own mind for more profitable researches, are "facetious" and "abstemious." Doctors go to bed—when they can, which isn't often—in the fond and sometimes desperate hope that they will be able to sleep, and the letters of the alphabet that visit their overburdened minds are cogent ones in familiar combinations, such as T.B. and E.S.P. It occurred to me that Dr. Conway, who had a hard time sleeping, might benefit by thinking dreamily of the letter Y and the soporific words for which it stands—yore and yarrow, youth and yesterday. Doctors, however, traditionally hunt for trouble, and all that Dr. Conway got out of Y was its noisy category of yammer and yell, yowl and yelp. This worried me, and I suddenly began thinking of myself as doctor and Conway as patient.

"N is probably the letter for you," I told him, "and I'm sorry I didn't prescribe it. But you know how it is; we have to proceed with each subject, or patient, by a process of trial and error. Some persons are nauseated by an injection of codeine—but react well to demerol. N should be fine for doctors of your temperament, because it is the letter of nowhere and never, novocain and nicotine and narcotic. If you drift into nightmare and nightshade instead of nightingale and narcissus, it is significant but not necessarily alarming. I worry about my doctors when they are undergoing alphabetical sedation only if they exhibit a tendency to slip too easily from nocturne and Nepenthe into some such sequelae as ninety naked night nurses." Dr. Conway seemed rather more disturbed than amused by my analysis of his association problems. "I don't know enough words beginning with N to get very far," he said.

"N doesn't have very many words," I said soothingly. "Practically nothing edible begins with N and there are almost no animals at all to keep you awake. So you won't lie there yearning for something to eat or worrying about beasts on the prowl. The newt and the narwhal cannot be said to prowl, but think of the animals that inhabit both sides of N, in M and O. The first has many creatures, from the mastodon to the mouse, and the second has an oppressively oleaginous company of oozy things, from the octopus to the oyster. But in N your consciousness is nurtured by the letter of Nineveh and Nirvana, No Man's Land and nomad, Nemo and Nod." Dr. Conway didn't say anything, he just went away. I understand that he takes sleeping pills now in order to sleep, and tries to think of nothing, including N.

I was perfectly content with my aimless wanderings in the avenues and lanes of the alphabet until Mr. Friedrich brought up the factor of value, or worth-whileness. When Dr. Alfred North Whitehead died, the *New York Times* described him as "a supreme adventurer in the realm of the mind." And now I am afraid that in its little piece about my own passing that great newspaper may refer to me as "just another vagabond in the backwoods of the imagination." This has taken the edge off my supine meanderings and given my dreams a nasty turn. In one of them I was being hunted down like a deer in a wooded wilderness. Men like Lord Bertrand Russell, another supreme adventurer in the realm of the mind, kept firing at me from cover. In something of a panic, I have recently been trying to give my nocturnal thoughts at least the semblance of importance. So far this has merely had the effect of making them a little stuffy. Whereas I used to drop off to sleep while looking for quiet characters in B, I now find myself trying to discover something significant in the curious ambivalence, the antipathy-affinity of C and M.

Most of the characters in B, to get back to them for a moment, murder sleep: the bugler, braggart, blowhard, blatherskite, barber, bowler, barker, booster, bouncer, bruiser, and so on. But their broken-bottle barroom brawling, bombast, bluster, and blockbusting bombardment of Babel and Bedlam die down when you come upon the subdued figures of the only truly quiet characters in the second letter of the alphabet—the butler, the bridegroom, and the burglar. The first night I came upon them, whispering and tiptoeing in the corridors of B, I fell asleep almost instantly. Now I lie awake for hours, staring at the ceiling, becoming more and more involved in what may easily turn out to be the utterly meaningless relationship of C and M. On the other hand, it is just barely possible that I have got the tips of my fingers on a valid and valuable discovery in the field of alphabetical relativity. I began, simply enough, with the discovery that C and M contain some of the greatest traditional antipathetical entities of fact and fiction—cat and mouse, cobra and mongoose, Capulet and Montague. From there I went on to explore certain other tragic associations of the two letters, Mary Celeste, Morro Castle, McKinley and Czolgosz, and Marat and Corday. I tried to get out of the darker side of the combination by thinking of Madonna and Child, Maurice Chevalier, and Christy Mathewson, but then I became wide awake and a little sweaty with Chamberlain and Munich, and Capitalism and Marxism, from which it was a simple mental journey to Christian and Moslem, civil and military, celibacy and marriage, church and monarchy, classical and modern, chemical and mechanical, mundane and cosmic. My mind had no sooner calmed itself with magic carpet than it leaped even wider awake with the Caine Mutiny and the Caine Mutiny Court Martial. I soon realized, as I turned on the lights and lit a cigarette, that C-M clearly militates against that relaxation of posture and thought which leads to unconsciousness. I got into dozens of conjunctions of the two letters—Mark and Cleopatra, Candida and Marchbanks, malice and charity, cow and moon, moth and cloth, mountain and climber, cadets and midshipmen, Monroe and colonization, and Custer and massacre. I began thinking of Charles Martel, who checked the Moors, but found this unrelaxing and tried to settle back in a cozy mental Morris chair. And suddenly I was in the midst of Martini cocktail, maraschino cherry, cockles and mussels, mutton chop, Château Margaux, mulled cider, Martell cognac, chocolate mousse, and Moët et Chandon. This naturally brought on cholera morbus. (Incidentally, the cholera morbus that killed Presi-

83

dent Zachary Taylor was caused by a surfeit of milk and cherries.) I don't know how I finally managed sleep; perhaps it was by thinking of the triumphs of the Count of Monte Cristo, or the whirling wheels of Monte Carlo, but my unconsciousness did not last long and my dreams were troubled. In one of them I was suddenly enfiladed by the rifle fire of the Coys and McHatfields. This distortion brought me so wide awake that I had to get up and dress.

A few nights later, having resolutely shaken C-M from my mind, I turned to S and W in the hope that the combination would be soft and winsome, soporific and wistful, but there is definitely a dark basic twist in my mental processes somewhere, for I abruptly shifted from a momentary contemplation of sweet William to storm warning, sou'wester, windstorm, waterspout, and shipwreck. I made a hasty grab for E, with its ease, ephemera, and evanescence, and then found myself, to my dismay, in the endless, eternal, everlasting, energetic enterprise and endeavor of the most restless letter of all twenty-six. Once you get into the explorations, examinations, excavations, and elaborate edifices of E, a tranquil mind is impossible. If you make the mistake of turning in desperation to D, you are even more disconcerted, for its doves, desires, and dreams give way almost at once to its terrible atmosphere of doubt, dread, decline, derangement, decay, dissolution, degradation, and its dire, dismal, disease, doom, and dusty death. If you contemplate the thousand depressing words that begin with D, you will understand why it was necessary to follow delightful and delicious with delovely in the Cole Porter song lyric. There just aren't three genuine

three-syllable words that would fit into the mood of ec-
stasy, so one had to be invented. If from this dark, dolorous,
demented, destructive, desperate, and demoniac letter you
look for serenity in F, you find yourself in both the frying
pan and the fire. F is the letter of falter, foozle, flunk, flop,
flaw, feeble, flounder, fall, flat, and failure, of fake, falla-
cious, flimflam, fishy, fib, fob, foist, forgery, facsimile, and
fabrication. The fox of its foxfire is not a fox, and the fire
is not fire. Even its fleabane is often false. It is the flimsy,
fluttery, finicky, frantic, frenetic, feverish headquarters of
flibbertigibbet, fuddyduddy, fogy, fossil, fourflusher, frus-
trated female, and flabbergasted fussbudget. To sports it
brings foul, fault, footfault, fumble, and forfeit. Its fineness
and finesse have a filigree frailty, and a furry fungus blurs
its focus, making it filmy, fuzzy, and foggy. When you
come upon fame, family, fortune, and faith in these sur-
roundings, they have a faint, furtive, fragile, and almost
fictitious feeling. F brings the fingers to butterfingers, the
fly to fly-by-night, the flash to flash-in-the-pan, and the for-
saken to godforsaken. Its friend is too close to fiend for
comfort, and it is not reassuring to realize that our finances
and future keep such fearful, fitful, fretful, and fantastic
company. F is so flagrantly flagitious and so flamboyantly
flexuous that it might easily drive any patient to floccilla-
tion, or at least make him want to rush out and flense a
whale with a fleam. If its fizzle doesn't get us, its fission
may.

G, if you are still with me, is no longer the most grue-
some, gloomy, and gory letter; its terrors have become old-
fashioned with the passing of the centuries and the

development of modern man. The things that go bump in G would no longer frighten even Goldilocks, for who is afraid nowadays of ghouls, ghosts, goblins, giants, gargoyles, griffins, gorgons, or Gargantua and Goliath? If you want to get hell's own heebie-jeebies, take H. This Century of Violence has invented new words and combinations of words and thrown a greenish light on old ones to point up its hellions and horrors, and most of them begin with H: hoodlum, hooligan, heel, hooch, heroin, hitchhiker, hotrod, hijacker, holdup, hophead, hipped, hideout, hatchetman, higher-up, hangover, hooker, homicide, homosexual, hydrogen, halitosis, hysteria, and Hollywood.

I don't know whether or not psychiatry has explored the diagnostic potential of what it would surely call, and perhaps already has, letter stimulus and word response. A simple way to measure the degree of apprehension, or *Angst,* in a patient who keeps looking over his shoulder or glancing into the sky would be the C-test or the T-test. I tried both of them on myself one night, with depressing results. All hell broke loose in each of them without warning. C has almost as many words of calm and comfort as of crisis and conflict, and the well-balanced psyche should be able to fall asleep while still in the category of anodyne, before the bells of alarm have begun to ring. I started out pleasantly and restfully one night like this: carillon, caroler, cavalcade, carriages, cobblestone, clip-clop, countryside, chickadee, candytuft, chimney corner, cricket, chessmen, cider, chestnuts. Then the trouble began, for C is the letter of catcall, curse, calumny, and contumely. I suddenly found myself in the midst of a loud-mouthed exchange of epithets and insults, from the old-fashioned cad and cockalorum up to the present-day card-carrying Communist conspirator and cockeyed Congressional-committee chairman. (If you can't fill in forty others, from clodhopper to creep, you are out of touch with your times.) The imprecations I had bumped into in C after such a serene start instantly led to creak, crack, crumple, crumble, collapse, crash, conflagration, consternation, confusion, cyclone, collision, calamity, catastrophe, cataclysm, and chaos. Anybody who can doze off while still thinking of clover, candle, comforter, clock, and chime is living in the alphabetical past, and his state of mind is probably even more indicative of derangement than my own.

There isn't a thing C can do that T cannot equal or surpass. I forget just how I started out in this promising letter of time and truth, but in a flash I was wandering among turtles and toadstools, and then I came to the tiny termite and what happened was far more terrible than the crackup in the chimney corner of C: tremble, teeter-totter, tower, tremor, tremblor, television, telephone, telegraph, transmission, topple, tumble, twist, topsy-turvy, tumult, turbulent, turmoil, thunder, tempest, tornado, tropical, typhoon, terror, tantrum, tirade, tailspin, traffic tieup, train, taxi, truck, trolley, tram, terminal, trouble, trial, tears, tribulation, torment, torture, triumph. (I don't know how that triumph got in there, but probably my consciousness had taken as much as it could.)

It is my intention to be helpful as possible to my neighbors at the corner of Dread and Jeopardy, and I suggest that they play around in P before venturing into more menacing letters. P is a rather silly letter, given to repeating itself, and to a strange assortment of games: ping-pong, polo, pool, poker, pedro, pinochle, parcheesi, pussy-wants-a-corner, post office, and pillow. The sixteenth letter of the alphabet has many pixies, great and small: Puck, Pan, Pandora, Peter Pan, Pinocchio, Pollyanna, Puss in Boots, and the Pooh. No other letter is quite so addicted to the vice of alliteration, and it is possible that no writer has ever lived who did not think up and mull over in his mind at least one title in the same category as *Pilgrim's Progress, Pippa Passes, Pied Piper, Pickwick Papers, Peterkin Papers, Pride and Prejudice, Prince and Pauper, Poet and Peasant, Pit and Pendulum, Peacock Pie, Potash and Perlmutter,* and so on, and on, and on, back through the ages. I once made up a little man named Pendly in the early years of my constant need to make money, and for some reason or other, no longer clear to me, I invented the name of a make of automobile in the same story. Naturally, I fell into the facile trap of repeating the P in the title of the story, which came out "Mr. Pendly and the Poindexter." It is because of this confounded tendency that our language is spotted with such expressions as pooh-pooh, pitter-patter, pish-posh, pompon, pretty please, postprandial, party politics, pumpkin papers, pink pills, pale people, pip-pip, pawpaw, papa, and the awful like.

In conclusion—all this thin slicing is getting us nowhere —easily the most fecund and probably the least frightening combination of letters is S-P. I have been working on it for years, off and on, and it has taken me from Stony Point to Seven Pines and from swimming pool to South

Pacific, with hundreds of stopoffs along the way. To games, for example, it has given southpaw, screen pass, short putt, set point, shot put, Sunday punch, and "sorry partner." Nothing has leaped out of this union to scale my pajamas off or to keep me awake very long. Right now, however, I am finding it a somnolent experience to wander in W, with its wilderness, Wonderland, wabe, wildwood, and Woodland of Weir. If you're lucky you can stay with nothing worse than witches and warlocks until the sandman gets you.

Pleasant dreams.

12

The Wings of
Henry James

One night nearly thirty years ago, in a legendary New York *boîte de nuit et des arts* called Tony's, I was taking part in a running literary gun fight that had begun with a derogatory or complimentary remark somebody made about something, when one of the participants, former Pinkerton man Dashiell Hammett, whose *The Maltese Falcon* had come out a couple of years before, suddenly startled us all by announcing that his writing had been influenced by Henry James's novel *The Wings of the Dove*. Nothing surprises me any more, but I couldn't have been more surprised then if Humphrey Bogart, another frequenter of that old salon of wassail and debate, had proclaimed that his acting bore the deep impress of the histrionic art of Maude Adams.

I was unable, in a recent reinvestigation, to find many feathers of *The Dove* in the claws of *The Falcon,* but there are a few "faint, far" (as James used to say) resemblances. In both novels, a fabulous fortune—jewels in *The Falcon,* inherited millions in *The Dove*—shapes the destinies of the disenchanted central characters; James's designing woman Kate Croy, like Hammett's pistol-packing babe Brigid O'Shaughnessy, loses her lover, although James's Renunciation Scene is managed, as who should say, rather more exquisitely than Hammett's, in which Sam Spade speaks these sweetly sorrowful parting words: "You angel! Well, if you get a good break you'll be out of San Quentin in twenty years and you can come back to me then." Whereupon he turns her over to the cops for the murder of his partner, Miles Archer (a good old Henry James name, that). Some strong young literary excavator may one day dig up other parallels, but I suggest that he avoid trying to relate the character in *The Falcon* called Cairo to James's early intention to use Cairo, instead of Venice, as the major setting of his novel. That is simply, as who should not say, one of those rococo coincidences.

The Wings of the Dove is now fifty-eight years old, but it still flies on, outward bound for the troubled future. Since 1902, it has become a kind of *femme fatale* of literature, exerting a curiously compelling effect upon authors, critics, playwrights, producers, and publishers. Seemingly, almost every playwright, from hack to first-rate talent, has been burned by the drama that glows within the novel's celebrated triangle, and has taken a swing at adapting it for stage or screen, usually with less than no success. It was James's own original intention to present his plot and characters in play form, but guardian angel or artist's insight caused him wisely to refrain from diverting into the theatre his delicately flowering, slowly proliferating history of fine consciences, which belongs so clearly between covers and not between curtains.

This doesn't keep people from adapting it, though. In 1956, Guy Bolton made a play out of it, *Child of Fortune*, which was produced on Broadway by the usually canny Jed Harris, who had earlier touched with art ("art schmart," he himself once disdainfully called it) his directing of *The Heiress*, based on Henry James's novel *Washington Square*. The Bolton *Dove* died miserably after twenty-three performances. That debacle did not deter television's *Playhouse 90* from having a go at dramatizing the novel just last year. This adaptation, made by a young man named Meade Roberts, seemed to me closer to the James tone and mood, closer to perfection of total production, than any other dramatization I have seen, and I have seen plenty. (The first one I ever encountered was shown to me by a young professor of English in Ohio forty-one years ago.) The success of *The Dove* on television lay in a discipline that gave it Henry James's key and pitch, if not his depth and range. Because my sight has failed, I could not see Inga Swenson, who played Milly, and this was probably fortunate, since I was told she looked as healthy as one of Thomas Hardy's milk-maids. But her words fell persuasively upon the ear, and she was the dying Milly to me. The direction gave the play a proper unhurried pace ("sluggish," wrote one restless newspaper critic), and there were moving offstage effects—the sound of distant bells in one scene, the haunting cry of gondoliers in another.

In my own college years, 1913-17, the literature courses in the modern English novel that were offered west of the Alleghenies included Hardy and Meredith, and sometimes Trollope, Samuel Butler, and Conrad, but rarely James. My own professor in this field, the late Joseph Russell Taylor, of Ohio State, rated James higher than the rest, and assigned *The Wings of the Dove* as required class reading, with this admonition: "If you can't make anything at all out of the first hundred pages, don't let it worry you." It was James's method to introduce his principal characters late, or, as John McNulty once put it, "to creep up on them in his stocking feet." Since only about one student in every thirty could stand, or understand, Henry James's writing, there were few persons with whom you could discuss the Old Master in those years. It was in 1930 that the Modern Library first introduced Henry James to its readers, with its edition of *The Turn of the Screw*, which has sold to date ninety thousand copies. The so-called Henry James Revival did not take place until the nineteen-forties, and centered on the hundredth anniversary of his birth. In 1946, the Modern Library brought out *The Wings of the Dove*, which has sold more than forty-one thousand copies. In 1958, *The Dove* lost its American copyright and fell into the public domain, and in January, 1959, Dell's Laurel edition of paperbacks printed seventy-five thousand copies of the novel, a little more than two-thirds of which either were sold or are out on the newsstands or in the bookstores.

The James Revival deserves the capital "R," because the increased sales of his books and the rapidly expanding literature on the man and his life and his work began crowding library shelves all over the country. In 1932, I bought the complete 1922 edition of James, issued by Macmillan of London, but it had not been easy to find. It was available in no New York bookstore then, and I finally got my set through a collector. It came from a private library on Park Avenue, which was then being sold, and not a single page of any of the more than thirty volumes had been cut. It was as if the owner of this particular edition had said, "I want to buy about two and a half or three feet of the works of Henry James." Interest in the Revival spread from Broadway to Hollywood. For years, David O. Selznick held the movie rights to *The Dove*, but he never produced an adaptation of the novel, unquestionably because of the difficulty of casting the three principal roles and of finding an adapter who could satisfactorily cope with the dramatization.

This seems the right place to describe briefly the "game," as James called it, that is afoot in his masterpiece.

Kate Croy, then, an ambitious young Englishwoman, emotionally intense and deeply amorous (James dresses her in such words as "ardor," "desire," and "passion"), is eager to marry a struggling young writer and journalist, Merton Densher in the novel but, mercifully, Miles Enshaw in the television play. Having developed, because of a penniless life with a wastrel father, what would now be called a neurosis or psychosis, Kate, with her "talent for life," is determined to enjoy money and marriage, and neither without the other. Into her predicament and pre-occupation drifts the American girl Milly Theale, attractive, enormously wealthy, naïve, and genuine, but perceptive ("mobile of mind"), in the best Henry James tradition, and dying. She falls in love with Densher, and the possessed, designing Kate perceives how she can use Milly's situation for her own selfish ends. She deliberately throws Milly and Densher together in Venice, and then reveals her scheme to him. He shall marry Milly, thus killing, you might say, two doves with one stone—Milly's final months on earth will be made happy ones, after which Kate and Densher will live happily ever after on the dead bride's millions. But Milly, again true to the James tradition of innocent American girls entangled in European society intrigue, discovers the true situation—that Kate is in love with and secretly engaged to Densher and that Densher is in love with Kate. Milly dies and, in her "copious will," leaves much of her wealth to the lovers, but they can never be happy with it, or without it. They are shadowed and separated forever by the wings of the dead dove, by the presence of a girl who is gone but everlastingly there.

Lest my oversimplification in this summary cause the ghost of Henry James to pace and mutter, I shall let him insert here a typical elucidation of the "conspiracy" of Kate and Merton: "The picture constituted, so far as may be, is that of a pair of natures well-nigh consumed by a sense of their intimate affinity and congruity, the reci-

95

procity of their desire, and thus passionately impatient of barriers and delays, yet with qualities of intelligence and character that they are meanwhile extraordinarily able to draw upon for the enrichment of their relation, the extension of their prospect and the support of their 'game.' "

There has probably been no other major novelist whose work has been so often criticized not so much for what it is but for what certain critics think it should have been. One critic, whose name I do not know, becoming impatient of the carpers, once said that they criticized Henry James as they might criticize a cat for not being a dog. These carpers are given to attacking, at the same time, the involved James style and his viewpoint on love, sex, women, affairs, and marriage. One reviewer of the *Playhouse 90* production insisted that no woman as passionately in love as Kate would hand her lover over to another woman, even temporarily, however great the promised compensation. The sensitive novelist never got used to the assaults upon him—understandably enough, for many of them were brutal. He was accused of "bombinating in a vacuum" and, by H. G. Wells, of laboring like a hippopotamus trying to pick up a pea. It was not a pea but a pearl, a James defender pointed out, and the hippopotamus had unbelievably skillful fingers.

As James's novels everywhere show, and his prefaces repeatedly declaim, he was caught unceasingly between the urge to "dramatize! dramatize!" and his passion for indirection—an ambivalence that must present both challenge and handicap to the adapter, however ingenious, of his work. In the last chapter of *The Dove,* James observes

that walks taken by Kate and Densher were "more remarkable for what they didn't say than for what they did."
The book ends with a hopeless headshake by Kate and
then the final speech "We shall never be again as we
were!," which is scarcely the way a born dramatist would
bring down his third-act curtain. And what can the helpless adapter do when confronted, as he frequently is, by
such lines as this: "The need to bury in the dark blindness
of each other's arms the knowledge of each other that they
couldn't undo." Incidentally, few artists with the physical
ability to see appreciate the truth known to all those without sight, that there is a dark blindness and a lighted
blindness. Henry James was at home in the dark and in
the light and in the shadows that lie between.

The theme of *The Dove* had germinated in what Edmund Wilson has called James's "marvellous intelligence"
(and Wells his "immensely abundant brain") upon the
death of a first cousin extremely dear to him, Minny
Temple, who departed his world and our world (they are
in many ways distinctly different) at the age of twenty-
four. He became so absorbed in his theme that he was
moved to prefigure Milly's death as dragging everybody
and everything down with it, like a great ship sinking or
a big business collapsing. This massive contemplation of
effect belongs to the mind and scheme of the novelist, but
it can't very well be encompassed in a dramatization, because one can't get stream of consciousness into a three-
act play. It is a commonplace of the ordeal of Henry
James that the presentation of his work on the stage, to
which he devoted many years, has been invariably better

managed in the theatre by other hands than his own. A few years ago, *The Turn of the Screw* was turned into *The Innocents,* and much earlier the unfinished novel *The Sense of the Past* shone upon the stage as *Berkeley Square.* Among the failures on Broadway ("It didn't just close, it flew closed," said Richard Maney) was an adaptation, nearly four years ago, of James's *The Europeans,* called *Eugenia* and starring Tallulah Bankhead, of whom Louis Kronenberger wrote, in a preface to his *Best Plays of 1956-57,* "only Mae West as Snow White could have seemed more unsuited to a part." Finding an actress, however gifted, who can play a Henry James woman convincingly must be a nightmare to any producer. One such rare lady is Flora Robson, who starred in London as Tina in Sir Michael Redgrave's recent dramatization of *The Aspern Papers,* a substantial hit and, I am told by a man who has seen them all, the finest presentation of a James work ever brought to the stage.

It had always seemed a wonder to me, until I got involved myself, that practically everybody wanted to write about *The Dove.* In the preface to the new paperback edition, R. P. Blackmur says, "By great luck I had been introduced simply and directly, and had responded in the same way, to what a vast number of people have thought an impossible novel by an impossible author and a vast number of other people have submitted to the stupefying idolatry of both gross and fine over-interpretation." Recently, Dr. Saul Rosenzweig, a psychologist and student of Henry James, dug up the opinion of the novelist-psychiatrist Dr. S. Weir Mitchell: "I have read his

[H.J.'s] last book with bewildered amazement. Since I played cat's cradle as a child, I have seen no tangle like it. To get the threads of his thought off his mind onto mine with the intermediation of his too exasperating style has been too much for me. A friend of mine says his 'Wings of a Dove' [sic] are unlike any dove she ever saw, for it has neither head nor tail. However, I am too old to learn a new language and still struggle to write my own with clearness."

Dr. Rosenzweig discovered a reply to the Mitchell objections in the correspondence of Owen Wister, creator of *The Virginian* and of the sundown gun duel on the deserted Western main street. "Henry James is in essence inscrutable," Wister wrote to Mitchell, "but one thing of him I know: our language has no artist more serious or austere at this moment. I explain to myself his bewildering style thus: he is attempting the impossible with it—a certain very particular form of the impossible; namely, to produce upon the reader, as a painting produces upon the gazer, a number of superimposed, simultaneous impressions. He would like to put several sentences on top of each other so that you could read them all at once, and get all at once the various shadings and complexities, instead of getting them consecutively as the mechanical nature of his medium compels. This I am sure is the secret of his involved parentheses, his strangely injected adverbs, the whole structure, in short, of his twisted syntax. One grows used to it by persisting. I read *The Ambassadors* twice, and like it amazingly as a prodigy of skill. One other thing of signal importance is a key to his later books.

He does not undertake to tell a story but to deal with a situation, a single situation. Beginning (in his scheme) at the center of this situation, he works outward, intricately and exhaustively, spinning his web around every part of the situation, every little necessary part no matter how slight, until he gradually presents to you the organic whole, worked out. You don't get the organic whole until he wishes you to and that is at the very end. But he never lets the situation go, never digresses for a single instant; and no matter how slow or long his pages may seem as you first read them, when you have at the end grasped the total thing, if you then look back you find that the voluminous texture is woven closely and that every touch bears upon the main issue. I don't say that if I could I would work like this, or that the situations he chooses to weave into such verbal labyrinth are such as I should care to deal with so minutely and laboriously, even if I had the art to do so; but I do say that judged as only any works of art can ever be judged; viz., by *themselves*, by what they undertake to do and how thoroughly they do it, Henry James' later books are the work of a master. . . ."

Wolcott Gibbs, to get back to the Guy Bolton adaptation of *The Dove*, found *Child of Fortune* ineffably tedious and dull, and Louis Kronenberger concluded that *The Dove* on the stage "can only succeed as something quite trashy or as something truly tremendous." It can, that is to say, succeed only on the scale of soap opera—*Milly Faces Life, Death Can Be Bountiful, The First Mrs. Densher, Wings of Riches*—or on that of grand opera, with such arias as "O gentle dove!," "This heart to thy swift flight," "Fold now thy tender wings," "Ah, passion but an hour!"

Thus, Meade Roberts's *Playhouse 90* dramatization was a unique achievement. I sat before my television set that night last year hoping for the passable, fearing the worst.

The worst is a perverse tendency, exhibited by at least one adapter in the past, to twist the plot into low, ironic comedy by saving the life of Milly Theale. Densher, that is, marries the rich girl only to find, to his dismay, and that of Kate, that Milly becomes a rose, no longer choked in the grass but fresh-sprung in the June of salutary happiness. We are a sentimental, soft-hearted nation, prone to lay violent hands upon death in art by calling in play doctors and heroine specialists of the kind that "saved" the doomed Lena, of Joseph Conrad's *Victory,* forty years ago, when it was made into a silent movie that was a combination of Pollyanna and Jack Holt. This saving of heroines, for a more recent instance in another sphere, was rudely accomplished by the Andrews Sisters in the case of the old Irish ballad "Molly Malone." The ballad has it that "She died of a fever and no one could save her," but the sympathetic Andrews Sisters did save her by cutting out that line, fitting her up with an artificial husband, and removing "Now a ghost wheels her barrow" and inserting "Now they both wheel her barrow," to the sorrow of millions who love Molly Malone not only alive, alive O, but dying and dead. When the resurrected Molly was crying her cockles and mussels over the airwaves a few years ago, I began fearing that the heroine specialists would go on to resurrect Shakespeare's Juliet, Verdi's Violetta, Wordsworth's Lucy, Browning's Evelyn Hope, Tennyson's Elaine, Poe's Annabel Lee, and Hemingway's Catherine Barkley. My fears gave rise to a terrifying nightmare in which I picked up a copy of *A Farewell to Arms* to discover that its title had been changed to *Over the Fever and Through the Crise*. It was during this period of apprehension that I went about muttering "I am mending, Egypt, mending." But *Playhouse 90*, bless its young heart, let Milly Theale die in the beauty of the Henry James lilies.

The profound and lasting effect upon Henry James of Minny Temple's untimely death shows up in many ways and places in his novels and stories. The simple, faintly comic name Minny Temple is reflected not only in Milly Theale but, in varying degrees, in the names of such other James heroines as Maggie Verver; Maisie, of *What Maisie Knew;* Mamie Pocock; Daisy Miller; May Bartram; Maria Gostrey; and Mary Antrim. Even Madame la Comtesse de Vionnet was named Marie. More than one of the girls in this "M" category die in the novels and novellas. I have set down the foregoing names from memory, and I am sure a research through the books would turn up many more. Probably dozens of seniors in English literature courses— like one I met at Yale a few years ago—have devoted their theses to a study of the proper names in Henry James. He had something more than a gift, almost an impish perversity, for the invention of plain, even homely feminine names, and by no means all of them were for his American women. The weediest of all is, I think, Fleda Vetch, of *The Spoils of Poynton*. As for his best-known American females, only a few, such as Isabel Archer and Carolina Spencer, do not grate upon the ear. This is partly because the voices of American women, from coast to coast, as he once said, were a torture to his own ear. Some fifty years ago, in *Harper's Bazar* (this was before it became *Harper's Bazaar*), he wrote half a dozen pieces about the speech and manners of the American Woman, which have never been brought together in any book. They might conceivably throw some light upon the James names for women, and upon his complicated, ambivalent attitude toward the ladies themselves. In any case, he usually took them up tenderly, fashioned so slenderly, young and so rich. What feminine reader has not wept over the death of poor dear Daisy Miller? And what sensitive gentleman can read the closing pages of *The Beast in the Jungle* and ever forget the anguish of John Marcher, to whom nothing whatever had happened, who through life had love forgone, quit of scars and tears but bearing the deep, incurable wound of emptiness? This story tells the tale of its author's loss of "the wings of experience," the burden and beauty and blessing of the love of a woman—something that was denied to Henry James for a complex of reasons, upon which the Freudians, especially during the nineteen-thirties, liked to get their eager fingers. Basically, he deliberately chose a loveless life because of his transfiguring conviction that the high art he practiced was not consonant with marriage but demanded the monastic disciplines of celibacy. He loved vicariously, though, and no man more intensely and sensitively.

It has always seemed to me that Henry James plunged

into the theatre to escape, perhaps without conscious intention, from the lifelessness of the silent study and the stuffy ivory tower. But no one can simply, or romantically, account for any novelist's taking on the theatre at intervals. There is always the lure of contact with an audience and the immediate response of appreciation, and there is also always what James called "the lust of a little possible gold." He supported himself by his writings, and he had the hope of making a killing on the stage for the sake of his budget and coffers. What resulted was an unequal struggle—his "tussle with the Black Devil of the theatre." He wrote a dozen plays in all, but only four were produced, and none were outstanding, and none made any money to speak of. And around him, all the time, bloomed, to his envy and usually to his disdain, such successes by his colleagues as *The Second Mrs. Tanqueray, An Ideal Husband,* and *The Passing of the Third Floor Back.* James's theatre pieces have been collected by Leon Edel, one of the most eminent living Jamesians, in *The Complete Plays of Henry James.*

Edel's swift and fascinating account of what was probably James's most hideous hour, the first night of his play *Guy Domville,* at the St. James's Theatre, in London, one January night in 1895, is itself worth the price of the volume. What happened that terrifying night would take too long to tell, and could not be done by anyone as well as Edel has done it. The evening might have grown out of the conjoined imaginations of Agatha Christie, Ed Wynn, and Robert Benchley. It began with the receipt of a mysterious telegram of bad wishes, and, after a compelling first act, abruptly changed gear and color in the second, with the entrance of an actress wearing a strange and comical hat. If James had, up to that night, still toyed with the idea of dramatizing the story of Milly Theale, he must have given up all thought of such a venture the moment he was dragged out upon the stage, at the end of the play, to the boos and catcalls that dominated the applause of an audience containing, among its host of celebrities, three comparatively unknown literary men—Arnold Bennett, H. G. Wells, and George Bernard Shaw. Incidentally, there have been few literary feuds so fascinating, and few so voluminously documented, as that between James and Wells, the introvert against the extrovert, the self-conscious artist versus the social-conscious novelist. The history of this long bicker and battle has been done by Edel and Gordon N. Ray in their *Henry James and H. G. Wells,* published, in 1958, by the University of Illinois Press.

Admirers of literature's hippopotamus with the skillful fingers and the sensitive soul must always mourn his having missed *The Heiress* and *The Innocents* and *Berkeley Square,* but their sorrow is compensated for by a sense of relief that he didn't have to experience the rigors and rigidities of Broadway. Anybody can survive editors and publishers, one way or another, but it takes the constitution of a Marine sergeant major to stand up under the bombardment of producers and directors, not to mention actors and actresses. Ellen Terry once promised to appear in a Henry James play in America, but never did, with the result that he called her "perfidious." He did manage to get the great Forbes-Robertson to appear in a play of his, but it is a now forgotten *succès d'estime,* a dim footnote to the record of that actor's achievements in the theatre. Once, James decided to turn a long one-act play of his into three acts by "curtain drops," dividing it into what he called stanzas or cantos. I can see now the faces of Jed Harris, Herman Shumlin, and Kermit Bloomgarden listening to the Old Master's "polysyllabic ponderosities" about *that.*

I think it is safe to say that television's voracious gobbling up of the literature of the past, which it regurgitates as Westerns, will leave Henry James's works uneaten, and even unbitten. There are now so many Westerns on television that their writers may soon be forced to adapt even the more famous Bible stories, and we may expect before long a bang-bang based on this distorted text: "Whither thou goest, I will go, God and the Cheyennes willing."

Until his untimely death, John Lardner, head of *The New Yorker's* department of television investigation, viewed with sound alarm and insight the Westernizing, among other things, of de Maupassant's sardonic classic "Boule de Suif," in which the fat French prostitute of the original was transmutilated into a slender and virtuous Apache princess, while quotations from Shakespeare flowered all over the desert till Hell wouldn't have it. That distortion of an indestructible piece of literature alarmed me, too, coming, as it did, only nine days after my happily groundless fears about the debauching of Henry James's *Dove.* When de Maupassant's famous coach was diverted from its journey between Rouen and Le Havre and re-routed across the Indian country, I began fretting about

106

what might happen to other celebrated coaches of literature—the one in *Vanity Fair*, all those that rumble through Dickens, and even the one that carries Cinderella to the ball. Then I began worrying about Lewis Carroll's coachless Alice. I could see her being driven, behind four horses, from a ladies' finishing school in Boston to California in order to be joined in unholy matrimony with a disturbed ex-haberdasher, one Mat Hadder, now a deranged U.S. marshal. Down from the hills, at the head of his howling tribe, sweeps Big Chief White Rabbit, but out of the West, the Farfetched West, to the blare of bugle music, rides Captain Marston ("March") Hare, who falls in love with Alice through the gun smoke, and—Ah, the hell with it. (For the sake of the record, it should be noted, in passing, that "Boule de Suif" was once dramatized for Broadway, with reasonable reverence, in a play called *The Channel Road.*)

I keep thinking of other possible—nay, probable—television corruptions: *Trelawny of the Wells Fargo, Lady Windermere's Gun, She Shoots to Conquer, Fanny's First Gunplay,* and even *The Sheriff Misses Tanqueray.* This Tanqueray is the fastest draw in English literature, and can outshoot the notorious desperado Long Gun Silver (and a high-ho to you, Long Gun, says I). To get all this frightening phantasmagoria off my mind, I have begun rereading, and hiding in, Henry James's *The Sacred Fount,* a story that will, I feel sure, forever foil the bang-bang transmutilators. For such small and negative blessings let us thank with brief thanksgiving whatever gods may be.

One thing that I can't yet dismiss from my waking thoughts and dawn dreams is the impish, tongue-in-cheek compulsion of the Western televisionaries to commingle the Bard and the bang-bangs. The other morning, I woke up with this line, from *Have Gun, Will Shakespeare,* chasing through my head: "How sweet the moonlight sleeps upon this—*bang!*"

Thataway, stranger, lies madness, so let us iris out on a quieter and safer area.

H. G. Wells, long-time friend and finally enemy of Henry James, once wrote, "For generations to come a select type of reader will brighten appreciatively to 'The Spoils of Poynton,' 'The Ambassadors,' 'The Tragic Muse,' 'The Golden Bowl' and many other stories." His prophecy was right, if you change "type" to "types," but his list of the stories he apparently liked best himself is unconvincing to me. I doubt, for instance, whether he ever got through *The Golden Bowl,* but if he did he left me somewhere in the middle of it. It is hard to understand how he could have left out the most controversial of all James's creations, *The Turn of the Screw.*

The undiminished power of the great "ghost story," after more than sixty years, was proved again, this time on television, when Ingrid Bergman starred in a dramatization by James Costigan, put on by the Ford *Startime* series just last year. I put "ghost story" in quotes because of the controversy that still rages, as rage goes in literary and psychological circles, about the true meaning of the narrative. Critical minds, in practically all known areas

108

of research and analysis, have got answers, dusty and otherwise, when hot for certainties in this, one of the greatest of all literary mysteries. Even with a merely competent cast, it would be hard to mar, or even dilute, the effectiveness of any dramatization, but Miss Bergman brought a memorable performance to a well-written, well-directed *Turn of the Screw*. She was equaled in every way by the performances of Alexandra Wager and Hayward Morse, as the two children of the eerie household.

One New York critic called it an "honest to God ghost story," and most viewers must indeed have been haunted and chilled by the strange goings-on in the great house of the wide circular staircase and the gloomy corridors. Dramatic and theatrical effectiveness aside, the question that has fascinated literary critics and psychoanalysts for six decades is this: Were the apparitions of the dead ex-governess, Miss Jessel, and of the violently dead ex-valet, Peter Quint, actual visitations from beyond the grave, or were they figments of the inflamed psyche of the new governess? The literature on the subject is extensive. Watchers of the television show who want to pursue the mystery into the library could turn to Edmund Wilson's "The Ambiguity of Henry James" in his *The Triple Thinkers,* James's own preface, and the narrative itself. Mr. Wilson pays tribute to Edna Kenton, one of the first psychographers to put forward the theory of hallucination instead of apparition. The James preface, in the manner of the Master, weaves a glittery web around his intention, at once brightening and obscuring it. He speaks of fairy tale and witchcraft, touches lightly on psychic research, and, of course, jumps over Freud completely. He can set so many metaphors and implications dancing at the same time on the point of his pen that it is hard to make out the pattern in the fluttering of all the winged words. I myself have never had the slightest doubt that he was completely aware of almost every latent meaning that has been read into the famous story. Henry James was not a student of Freud; he was a sophomore in psychology compared to his distinguished brother William, and I once read a letter of Henry's in which he somewhat pettishly dismissed the assumptions of Freud as akin to those of spiritualism. But when it came to pondering his plots, turning over his characters and incidents the way a squirrel turns over a nut, he was the pure artist, less susceptible than almost any other to unreasoned impulse.

Some years ago, in a little town in Connecticut, I had the pleasure of meeting, at a party, a gracious lady whose mother was the sister of Minny Temple. She told me a wonderful tale of something that happened at twilight in England many, many years ago, when she was a young girl. I like to think that the incident took place at the very time Henry James was working out, in his conscious mind, the tricks and devices of *The Turn of the Screw*. At any rate, the venerable figure of the distinguished novelist, wearing opera hat and cape, stood outside a house, in the fading light, and peered through a window at the young lady and one or two other girls, to give them what he might have called "the tiniest of thrills." And so to me, if to no one else, it is clear that this gave him the idea of the apparition, at a window, of the ghostly figure of Peter Quint.

Alas, I am now told that the gracious lady not only has forgotten the incident but does not believe it happened, and cannot recall telling me about it. And so this rambling flight into the past ends, as perhaps it should properly end, on a faint, far note of mystery.

13

Hark the *Herald Tribune, Times,* and All the Other Angels Sing

It probably just *seems* forever that I have been listening to and reading the Great Big Ballyhoo, over the air and in the papers, for Hollywood and Hell's Own Monumental in color called *The Conqueror,* a terribly expensive Hyper-Spectacular about Genghis Khan, who has "cowering nations under his heel, an untamed woman in his arms." (The role is played by John Wayne, the Ringo Kid of *Stagecoach.*) The shouting must have begun at least three months ago. Before that, radio, in its dying years, was already filling the day and night with screams, backed up by loud music and pistol shots, horribly reminiscent of ships going down at sea in lightning storms. "Listen! Listen! Listen!" a man kept crying every few minutes over WABC, and "Missing! Missing! Missing!" somebody bawled all the time over WMGM. It got me to waking up at night screaming "Murder! Murder! Murder!" And then along came *The Conqueror*, clamant and clangorous, trailing such a gaudy glory of boasts as has not exacerbated my

ears since God moved Cecil B. de Mille to make *The Ten Commandments*.

The only quiet note in the whole prolonged business was the small voice of an innocent French spectator of the movie, when it had a preview in Paris some months ago. I happened to turn on the radio one day in time to hear a representative of the *Conquerissimo* interviewing people as they came out of a Paris theatre. "What did you think of it?" he demanded breathlessly of this Frenchman. "Good. Nice. I don't speak much," murmured the Frenchman politely. I love that Frenchman and hope someday to buy him a Pernod.

After that, it was just yelling and screaming all the time. It may still be going on, for all I know. I flew to Bermuda to get away from it all, and am writing this jittery memoir down there, expecting any minute that men in white coats will come for me. I still keep shouting in my sleep, and can often be heard hollering great big adjectives around the house in the daytime, wild of eye, tousled of hair. What finally drove me to flight was the *New York Times* which contained a double-page ad for a brand-new Undreamed-Of Magnificent called *Alexander the Great.* You couldn't have missed it unless you were in the hospital or solitary confinement, but for the sake of the record, its screaming began like this: "THE COLOSSUS WHO CONQUERED THE WORLD. ALEXANDER THE GREAT. NOW . . . THE COLOSSUS OF MOTION PICTURES! PEOPLED WITH A CAST OF THOUSANDS! IN PREPARATION FOR OVER A DECADE! SO MIGHTY IT STAGGERS THE IMAGINATION!"

I have a feverish, distorted memory of the rest of the Revolution, which seemed to take in every passion, battle, march, and phenomenon from the *Anabasis* to *The Seven Pillars of Wisdom.* The Untamed Woman in the Conqueror's Arms disappeared like a feather in a snowstorm when the boys got through with their ballyhoo for the new

114

Incredible. "The Debauched Grecian Maidens . . . The Mass Marriage of Thousands of Persian Women!" the *Times* ad said, with a leer startlingly unfamiliar in the pages of that austere journal. (That last exclamation point is mine, and it may be the only private one left in the East.)

I had to do something heroic to exorcise the howling devils of my nightmares, and so, as the recent Winter kept

eluding the hounds of Spring, adding a chill to the gloom of my thoughts, I would lie in bed and compose Screamer Streamers and Clangor Commercials for my own Super

Mammoth production, in Miracolor and Vastascreen, of Wordsworth's "Lucy." I picked out a wonderful star for the Titanic Title Role, one Bvuga Breen, an unheard-of new combination of Flesh and Spirit, Body and Soul, half Indonesian tigress, half Brooklyn housewife. I can't remember a tenth of the ads I wrote before my medical man and my psychiatrist began shaking their heads over my chart, but some of the more thunderous praises stick in my shaking mind. "The Loneliest Woman in the World! The One and Only Lucy of the Magnificently Empty Life, brought out from behind that Mossy Stone, a Violet like no other violet you ever heard of, half naked, half dirndl-clad. Supported by more than two million women, representing Every Woman—for Lucy, whose Epic has been in preparation since Wordsworth died, is You and You and You! She didn't know Anybody, she never did Anything, she never went Anywhere. Nobody more than fifty yards from the Springs of Dove (which cost a cool $750,000 to reproduce) had heard of Lucy. A Miracle of Solitude! The producers were staggered when they realized that Lucy must die without anybody except one man finding out about it. Then their millionaire writers came up with God's Own Solution. They made this man Every Man! He is You and You and You. What to do about the single star the old-fashioned poet had put in the sky above the untrodden ways? One writer fell dead of a surfeit of awe and envy when a colleague hit the Great Idea on the Head. In *Lucy*, the fair solitary star first shines all alone, and then, on the Vastascreen, which runs around all four walls of the theatre and up over the ceiling, more than a thousand billion stars suddenly glitter. They represent You and You and You, and You and You and You! Don't, for God's sake, miss Bvuga Breen in the sultry screen classic of the loneliest woman in the world, supported by practically everybody you ever heard of! Everybody you ever heard of, I tell you! Everybody in the world, do you hear me? Everybody in Hell, Hollywood, and Heaven, I tell you! DO YOU HEAR ME? DO YOU HEAR M

EDITOR'S NOTE: The unfinished manuscript ends abruptly, probably at the moment they came for him.

14

The New
Vocabularianism

A sensitive gentleman in one of Henry James's novels exclaims at the end, triumphantly, "Then there we are!" not because he and his fair companion have arrived at a solution of anything but because they have come upon an embraceable impasse.

The expression Embraceable Impasse (I stress it with capitals deliberately) might well become a part of the jargon of today's diplomacy, which so often seems content to settle for a phrase in place of a way out. One such phrase, Calculated Risk, has been going great guns among the politicians and statesmen. It was used repeatedly by an adult guest on an American radio discussion panel made up of juveniles. (I am glad and eager to announce that we have millions of teenagers in America more interested in using their minds than in brandishing knives or bicycle chains.) Finally one youth interrupted the adult to say "I don't know what you mean by Calculated Risk." The grown-up was as bewildered as if the youngster had said "I don't know whom you mean by Harry Truman." This particular Calculated Risk was being applied to the Russo-American plan of exchange students, and the adult guest floundered a bit in trying to explain what he meant.

Now I have made some study of the smoke-screen phrases of the political terminologists, and they have to be described rather than defined. Calculated Risk, then, goes like this: "We have every hope and assurance that the plan will be successful, but if it doesn't work we knew all the time it wouldn't, and said so."

There is, to be sure, a kind of menacing Alice in Wonderland meaninglessness in a great deal of modern political phraseology. What used to be called a tenable position could now often be called, quite fittingly, a Tenniel position. To add to the unmeaningfulness of it all, there is the continual confusing contribution of the abbreviationists. We have in America a product called No-Cal, short for No Calories, and another Decaf, meaning "coffee from which caffein has been removed." Before long, I fear, Calculated Risk will become Cal-Ris, and then all the other celebrated phrases will be abbreviated, for the sake of making even less sense than before in front-page headlines. We shall have to have a special glossary, perhaps, to help us figure out "Pea-Coex" and "Ag-Reapp" and "Mass-Retal." I should think even the most backward student of world affairs would understand "Sum-Con." Then the Marxist intel-

119

lectuals will hit them with those old brickbats called Obscurantism and Obfuscationism. The meaning of these two words will be described, in my own forthcoming dictionary, like this: "You are seeking to distort our objectives by exposing them to the scrutiny of the unfairest of all bourgeois virtues, namely truth."

Somewhere in my proposed lexicon I shall have to wedge in what a lady said to me when I told her I was writing a short piece about the time, if any, of Man on earth. She said, with a distressed sigh, "So much has already been written about everything that you can't find out anything about it."

The brain of our species is, as we know, made up largely of potassium, phosphorus, propaganda, and politics, with the result that how not to understand what should be clearer is becoming easier and easier for all of us. Sanity, soundness, and sincerity, of which gleams and stains can still be found in the human brain under powerful microscopes, flourish only in a culture of clarification, which is now becoming harder and harder to detect with the naked eye. My dictionary, in attacking or circling about the terminology of the declarificationists, will contain such directives as this, for the bewildermentation of exchange students on all sides: "When you find that they are superior to us in any field, remember that their superiority is inferior to ours."

Let us mourn for a moment the death of Latin in American high schools. That ancient sword of Cicero, lyre of Catullus, and thunder of Virgil has become the pallid valet of the lawyer and the doctor, laying out their double-breasted polysyllabics, workaday clichés, and full-dress circumlocutions. "I had to let my secretary go," a doctor told me. "She could never remember the Latin for cod liver oil." In my day, Latin was taught in high schools to prepare the youthful mind for the endless war between meaning and gobbledegook. But it was a mental discipline, and discipline has become a bad word in America, for the idiotic reason that we identify it with regimentation, and hence damn it as Communistic. Recent surveys in my country indicate that Latin and certain other difficult subjects were eliminated from school curricula because they were simply too hard for Junior and his sister to understand, and interfered with the coziness of their security. An aroused America is now, I am glad to say, interested in the rehabilitation of our declining educational system. We have long had, in our colleges and universities, easy courses variously known as snap, soft, cinch, and pudd, which seems to be short for "pudding." I asked a pretty girl graduate of the University of Kansas if she had taken any pudd courses, and she said she had taken two. Common Insect Pests and Native Shrubs and Trees. "They were so dull I failed them both," she told me.

The tendency of tired American businessmen and statesmen to use slang and slogan will, I hope, disappear with the revival of true education. When our recent President used the word "gimmick" for "political device" he seemed to open the door for a flood of Hollywood shibboleth. I can only pray that Washington does not fall into the use of "switcheroo" and "twisterino."

My concern about the precarious state of the English

language in the hands or on the tongues of politicians shows up in recurring nightmares. I dreamed one night I was at some kind of Sum-Con, and two famous lines, one English, the other American, became garbled slightly and unfortunately conjoined. They were Browning's "Beautiful Evelyn Hope is dead," and that proud boast of all New England inns, "George Washington slept here." They came out in my nightmare like this: "Beautiful Evelyn Hope is deaf. George Washington slapt her."

"Gentlemen, this means war," said a grave voice in my dream, and I woke up. It was hard to get back to sleep, and I thought many thoughts. I began worrying again about the death of Latin, and I said aloud, waking up my wife, "What does he know of English who only English knows?" The restoration of Latin in our schools is not going to save Man from himself, to be sure, but it would help in the coming struggle for a world regime of sense and sanity. *Hoc est,* at any rate, *in votis.*

15

The Saving Grace

"I have wanted to argue with you since 1951," said a woman who sat down next to me, around midnight, at a recent party in Connecticut.

"You have shown remarkable restraint for your impatient sex," I said. "Here it is 1961. What is it you want to be wrong about?"

"In 1951, in an interview, you said that humor would be dead within five years. Well, it wasn't," she said firmly.

"I said it would either be dead or off its rocker," I told her. "Perhaps it is both. You may have seen its gibbering ghost."

"Do you think ghosts are crazy?" she demanded.

"Well," I said, "anyone who rejoins our species, after once being quit of it, can scarcely be called bright, can she?"

Here she proved too quick for me. "It was Banquo who

made that awful scene in the dining room, not Lady Banquo," she pointed out. I could have observed that Lady Banquo was not dead, but it would have been too easy.

"Lady Banquo sent him there," I said. "You know how women ghosts are."

"I don't want to get into the First Folio, or anything like that," she said with a touch of irritation. "What did you think was the matter with humor in 1951?"

"It was suffering from acute hysteria, pernicious fission, recurring nightmare, loose talk, false witness, undulant panic, ingrown suspicion, and occlusion of perception—quite a syndrome," I said. "When reason totters and imagination reels, humor loses its balance, too."

"It is called the saving grace," she said, making a sharp left jab of the truism. I wasn't off guard, though.

"Grace can't save us unless we save it," I said.

"It *is* saved," she insisted. "It's on all sides of us. You just don't want to see it. What else do you think has happened to humor?"

"It suffers from chronic crippling statistics," I told her. "Humor flourishes only as a free single entity. Humor makes its own balances and patterns out of the disorganization of life around it, but disorganization has been wiped out by organization, statistics, surveys, group action, program, platform, imperatives, and the like. These are good for satire, but they put a strait jacket on humor."

A man with a highball glass in his hand wavered over to us and said to me, "You guys give me a pain in the neck. On the other hand, the pain in Twain stays mainly in the brain."

For such crude intruders I always carry a piece of complicated academic drollery, and I gave it to him: "If you prefer 'I think, therefore I am' to '*Non sum qualis eram*,' you are putting Descartes before Horace."

He hesitated, jiggling the ice in his glass. "Nuts," he said, and wove away.

"Who was that feeble-minded son of bombast and confusion?" I asked my companion.

"My husband," she said. "My name is Mrs. Groper. Alice Groper. Tell me some more about statistics, but not too much."

"Last Monday," I said, "I heard three news broadcasters say, '*Only* two hundred and sixty-two people were killed in automobile accidents in the past two days,' and one of them added that nearly a hundred people—eighty-eight, to be exact—were alive that might have been dead. He was basing his statistics on an estimated three hundred and fifty dead, confidently predicted by the Safety Council. In the place of humor, you see, we have grim, or negative, cheerfulness. One statistician not long ago tried to cheer us all with his estimate that only eighteen million people, not fifty million, would be killed here in a nuclear war. This kind of horrifying reassurance is now our main substitute for laughter."

"I don't want to talk about horrifying reassurance," said Mrs. Groper.

"Take teeth, then," I told her. "Last year, in London, somebody asked me why Americans thought teeth were so funny. I explained that it is not teeth, but the absence of teeth, that we regard as funny, and also the absence of hair."

"But we laugh at paunches, too," she cut in quickly, "and that's the presence of something."

"Not at all," I told her. "What we laugh at is the absence of the once flat abdomen. If I am splitting hairs, they are the hairs just above the male ears, as all the others are so hilariously gone."

"Let's not go into philosophy or definition," said Mrs. Groper. "They never get you anywhere."

"They have got us where we are, or, anyway, they have left us there," I said. "Now, disorganization must not be confused with disintegration. If the falling apart of the human body is funny, then death should be the biggest laugh of all. I think I saw this concept forming when the

edentulous mouth was first deemed to be uproarious. That was a long time ago, and I hoped that the comedy of dentures would disappear along with the jokes about the activities of Mrs. Eleanor Roosevelt, but I was wrong. Mike Nichols and Elaine May, and even the English playwright Graham Greene, regard teeth as highly amusing. The usually very humorous Nichols and May have a protracted, or perhaps I should say extracted, skit about a dentist who falls in love with the decayed molar of a young woman patient, and then with the rest of her. (They call her Reba, but I would prefer Sesame.) Mr. Greene's latest comedy success on the London stage concerns a love triangle involving a dentist, a bookseller, and the dentist's wife. In this play the dentist occasionally flashes his electric torch into his rival's mouth and warns him about a certain tooth. The play was a huge success, and I expect any day now to encounter a burlesque called *The Bridgework on the River Kwai.* I happen to consider the oral cavity to be about as humorous as a certain canal. Ask me, what canal?"

"What canal?" asked Mrs. Groper.

"Alimentary, my dear Watson," I said. "Why don't you giggle?"

"Because my name is not Watson, and I don't know what you're talking about," she said.

"I am talking about the fragmentation of the human organism as the source and subject of dubious fun," I said. "One August a weekly magazine I sometimes write for became avant-garde in this field of humor and came up with a comic drawing about the virus called Staphylococcus aureus. There were no funny drawings in the magazine about people, only about other creatures. The idea that persons, as such, in their entirety may be passing from the American comic scene keeps me awake at night. One dawn I woke up singing, 'When you were the fly in the ointment and I was the cat in the bag.' Then I worked out the caption for the drawing of a bug in a rug. It is saying to another bug, 'I can't get comfortable.' "

"But you have done a hundred fables about talking animals and birds," she reminded me. Having determined not to drink anything that night, I sipped my second highball slowly.

"You have mislaid your discriminator," I told her brusquely. "The fable form has immemorially *identified* the behavior of animals and birds with that of people, to emphasize the foibles and follies of the human race. But talking animals in cartoons are now tending to denigrate man by assuming attitudes of superiority. For example, you find two giraffes staring at a human being, and one of them is saying, 'There ain't any such animal.' Or a cartoon will show half a dozen persons on all fours with their heads buried in the sand, and one ostrich is saying to another, 'My God, look who's fallen for *that* old myth.' "

"Didn't anything funny at all, in the old-fashioned sense, happen to you while you were in Europe last year?" Mrs. Groper wanted to know. "I think you're just in a depressed mood. You've had too little to drink. I'll get you another highball," and she did.

"Well, there were the Hugginses," I said when she came back with the drink.

128

"Now, *that's* funny." She laughed merrily.

"Not frightfully," I said, "and yet it was frightful, too—what happened to them on the ship coming home, I mean."

"Did they fall overboard?" she asked.

"No, but they went off the deep end," I said. "Here's what happened. Mrs. Huggins had bought a new dress in Paris, at the most expensive shop—I'll call it Violetta's. While her husband was out on deck one day, staring at the sea and trying to remember how many people had gone down on the *Titanic,* not how many had been saved, she removed the label from the dress and sewed in the label of what you women call a reasonable shop, a small shop in New York. But it preyed on her mind, and so she later ripped out the label and put the Violetta one back in."

"That's not so funny," my companion said. "We all do things like that. We're all afraid of the customs inspectors."

"Anyway," I said, "my wife and I met the Hugginses for drinks one night after dinner on the ship. They had already had a lot of cocktails and wine, and they were both on the edge of their chairs. She was also on the edge of colitis, and he was threatened with a new ulcer."

"I don't see why, if she had sewed the real label back in," said my companion.

"It was this way," I said. "Huggins told his wife that any customs inspector would be able to tell that the Violetta label had been sewed into the dress by a nervous and amateur hand—that is, a guilty hand."

"So what?" demanded Mrs. Groper. "It belonged there."

"Belonging is a matter of congruity, not of simple fact," I explained. "The human mind, or mental state, being what it now is, the inspector would be sure to say, 'Madam, this is clearly not a Violetta dress. You have sewed the label of an expensive Paris shop into an inexpensive American-made dress that you obviously took to Europe with you.' "

"But why would Mrs. Huggins conspire with herself to pay duty on an imported dress when she didn't have to, if it wasn't really imported, even though it actually was?" Mrs. Groper asked.

"You're oversimplifying," I told her sharply. "The assumption would be that Mrs. Huggins was trying to get away with something. I mean, that she was willing to pay a hundred dollars in duty just to prove to her friends that her husband could afford a Violetta dress for her."

"What finally happened?" asked Mrs. Groper.

"Huggins wanted to throw the dress overboard," I said. "To save money, you see."

"Do I?" she asked.

"Certainly," I said. "If the case got to the courts as the result of Mrs. Huggins' determination to prove that the Violetta dress was in fact a Violetta dress, Violetta herself might have to be flown to New York to testify. Lawyers' fees, court costs, and so on would run into a pretty figure. Well, anyway, over our drinks that night, Mrs. Huggins burst into tears. My own wife, returning from the ladies' room at that moment, accused me of having hurt her feelings. That made *me* mad. Then suddenly Huggins smote the table with his right fist, breaking his glasses, which he had forgotten were there. His wife reached over impulsively and cut her right index finger on a fragment of broken lens."

"I think you're losing me now," my companion said.

"We're all lost," I said irritably. "When Mrs. Huggins' finger began bleeding, I yelled at her, 'Why in the name of God do you have to cut yourself every time your husband breaks his glasses?' You see, I was mad at her now because she had not denied that I had hurt her feelings. Humor had folded its tents like the Arabs and noisily stolen away from a situation that demanded its presence."

"Goatblather," said Mr. Groper as he passed my chair, jiggling ice cubes in a fresh highball.

"Your husband has all the charm of a gentleman I shall now tell you about," I said. "The story points up the decline of humor in our time and in our species. Recently two couples, entirely unknown to each other, were leaving a Broadway theatre at the end of the play. They were moving slowly and with difficulty up the crowded aisle, when the observant wife of one man whispered in his ear, 'You're unzipped!' He hastily zipped and, in so doing, caught in the zipper the fringe of the other woman's stole. The embarrassing predicament soon became uncomfortably obvious to all four. They were huddled together as they reached the curb, where the husband of the woman with the trapped stole said grimly, 'Let us not make a social occasion of this. We shall all get in the same cab and drive to whichever apartment is the nearer.' And they did just that, in gloomy silence."

"But," said Mrs. Groper, "they could have taken separate cabs, and the stole could have been returned next day."

"The husband of the stole," I explained, "made it clear that he did not want to exchange names with the other couple. When they got to the nearer apartment, the two gentlemen retired to another room, where they finally managed to extricate the stole. Then the two couples separated without so much as a good night."

"But if they had had a nightcap together, they all would have laughed about it," said Mrs. Groper. "You just can't be dignified in a situation like that. You need another drink." And she left to get me one.

"Keep it clean, Mac," said the peripatetic Groper, passing my chair again.

"Don't you ever sit down, for God's sake?" I yelled after him. His wife brought me the fresh drink, and I added a moral to the tale: "When dignity does not give, humor cannot live."

At this point my wife joined Mrs. Groper and me and said, "Why are you shouting?" I started to explain, realized that it couldn't be done, and sulked instead.

"Did Mr. Huggins finally throw the dress overboard?" Mrs. Groper asked my wife.

"Oh, that," my wife said. "Of course not. They were lucky. The customs inspector didn't even look at the dress."

The party was growing noisy now, and we could hardly hear one another. Someone had put a record on the phonograph, and several couples were dancing.

"If that's all there is to it," said Mrs. Groper, "it isn't really frightful unless Mrs. Huggins got blood poisoning and died."

"Oh, my God, I didn't know that!" my wife cried.

"We all have to go sometime," I yelled.

"I was ready to go an hour ago," my wife said, "but you were taking something apart, as usual."

"A woman always assumes that a man is taking something apart when he's trying to put it together," I said.

"We *must* go," my wife insisted.

"Not until I save Mrs. Huggins' life," I said. "It's the least I can do." But Alice Groper was no longer interested in the plight of the Hugginses.

"Your husband has been officiating at the burial of humor," she said.

"Oh, he has, has he?" said my wife. "Well, he defends humor just as often as he buries it. It all depends on whether he, or somebody else, is attacking it. Doesn't it?" she demanded.

"Yes," I said, grudgingly, pulling myself out of my funereal mood.

"Now you're making sense," said Mr. Groper, holding out his hand. I thought for a moment of biting it, but shook it instead. "How's about a little old toast to humor?" he asked. The music had stopped and the others in the room gathered around us.

"You do the honors," Mrs. Groper said to me. I stood up, without too much difficulty, and held my glass high.

"Here's to the Queen," I said. "The Queen of the graces." As we were drinking to the hardy survivor of centuries of American life, our hostess, a lady of great charm but small regard for syntax, cried, "Do not for the God's sake break the glasses! Too many glasses are broken already without toasting Queens, so it is enough, and not funny." Everybody thought it *was* funny, though, and everybody began laughing. My wife and I were leaving the jolly house, good humor all intact, the sound of merriment in our ears, when Groper came up and extended that damned right hand of his. I took it. "I'm sorry I mentioned your goatblather," he said. I wanted to throw him over my shoulder, but I am thirty years too old for that gesture in conclusion. "It is nannyblibberers like you that are full of goatblather," I told him.

"Come on!" my wife said, pulling me toward our car as if I were six years old, which, like all American adult males, I sometimes am.

When we were back in our living room she said, "Grief-stricken as you are by the death of humor, maybe a nightcap would put you in a better mood." I nodded, having never rejected a nightcap since 1915.

"I am, *au fond*, a mellow foxy grandpa-type philosopher," I told her. "While we finish the nightcap, I shall count your lucky blessings, name them one by one."

"Then," she said, "we'll only need a short drink." And she made us both a short one.

16

Come Across
with the Facts

"Do you believe that education in our time and nation is
going to improve?" lovely women often ask me at cocktail
parties.

"No, ma'am," I always reply, politely. "I think it is going
to hell."

"Upon what do you base those dark prognostics?" the
ladies, many of whom almost got through high school before they quit to get married, will demand.

"Upon letters that I get from boys and girls in the
eighth, ninth, tenth, eleventh and twelfth grades of schools
all over the country, asking me—nay, madam, ordering me
—to write their term papers for them."

"Don't you want to hear from these children, or what?"
asked Mrs. Quibble. (Let's call all these ladies Mrs. Quib-

ble, and put this thing in the past tense, before it drives me crazy.)

"Almost all the letters indicate that we are a nation of tired teachers and apathetic pupils," I said. "I gather that the English teachers cannot interest the children in any writer that isn't living. The youngsters seem to regard all dead writers, from Thackeray to Jim Tully, as equally dull. Dead writers do not send out autographs or autographed photographs. Before long the kids will begin asking a writer for a pencil he has used, or a button from his overcoat, to be sure of getting passing grades."

Mrs. Quibble looked puzzled and skeptical. "You are not making yourself precisive," she said. "You are digressionizing. What is it that's eating you, anyways?"

"May I get you a raspberry ice?" I asked courteously. "You have had too many martinis."

"Don't get cute," she said, with fine hauteur, reaching for another martini. "Give me some instances."

"Let me say first," I said first, "one out of every thirty-two letters shows a trace of originality, even a gleam of ingenuity. If statistics interest you, one out of five girls spells 'all right' 'alright.' "

"Well, if they spell all right, then all right," snapped Mrs. Quibble. "What's eating you, anyhow?"

"That's 'anyhows,' " I said. "Leastways, if it's 'anyways,' then it has to be 'anyhows.' "

"You choose to be egnimatic," said Mrs. Quibble. "As for spelling, my great-grandmother couldn't even read or write."

"And look at her now," I said severely. "Dead and gone

and forgotten by everyone on this planet save you."

"Never mind about saving me. You'd better save yourself. You're the one that needs saving," she told me. She reached for a martini on a tray, but I beat her to it.

"What disturbs me most," I said, offering her the olive, which she refused, "is the pervading apathy, the lengthening shadow of lethargy across the land. Almost everybody wants to get through school, or, rather, get *around* it, the easy way. It doesn't surprise me to learn that one can buy themes, theses, dissertations, stand-ins for exams, and even Ph.D. degrees."

"Let's get down to pacific instances about the letters you get from children," said Mrs. Quibble.

"Well, then," I said, "the average letter I get goes like this: 'I have read all your books and liked them very much, and your attitude toward life. Please answer the following questions. 1. What books have you written? 2. What is your attitude toward life? If you will answer this, I will get an A, maybe with a photograph of yourself. You are a Twentieth Century author, and so there is nothing about you in the libary.' One boy ended his letter with, 'Please process this information as soon as possible.'"

"There are worse things than that," Mrs. Quibble said, but she didn't name any. "Do you answer these children?"

"Only the ones that sound intelligent and sincere," I said. "Some of the children write from villages or ghost towns, and I believe them when they say there is no library where they live, or that it has no books that tell you anything about anybody since Tennyson. I have answered boys and girls in places like Wounded Knee,

137

South Dakota, and Dilles Bottom, Ohio, but I refuse to do any research work or writing for New York City children."

"Do you hear from *them?*" my companion wanted to know.

"Once in a while," I said. "I answered one young lazybones and told him he was a liar when he said there was nothing about twentieth-century writers in any New York library. Another New York youngster asked me how to dedicate a book. Since I figured he would never write a book, and probably couldn't tie his tie or shoes without help, I threw his letter away. Then I got another one from him, at once aggrieved and imperious, demanding to know how to dedicate a book. I told him."

"I suppose your letter was full of ironics," said Mrs. Quibble. This time she beat me to the martini on the passing tray.

"I told him that he could dedicate it 'To Mom,' or 'To Madge Mudge,' or 'To Pop,' but I suggested that if he ever did write a book, the most fitting dedication should probably go like this: 'To Miss Gorby, whom, without she had learnt me English, this book never would of been written.' "

"Nobody is as unliterate as that, and you know it," said Mrs. Quibble.

"They ain't, huh?" I said. "You should see my mail, which, without I got so much of it, I might of got more written."

I could tell from Mrs. Quibble's expression that she was seeking for a single sentence with which to destroy me and my subversive attitude toward American education. She found it at last.

"The trouble with you is, you just don't like no children," she said coldly.

"You are wrong, madam," I said icily. "I *do* like no children."

EDITOR'S NOTE: Mr. Thurber does like children, but he thinks nothing of abusing truth to point up a grammatical outrage.

17

The Case for Comedy

The robin in my apple tree sings as cheerily now as if he were living in the Gay Nineties, when there never was a cakewalk or a band concert in the park that ended in a knife fight, the throwing of beer cans and bottles, the calling out of the National Guard, and the turning of fire hoses on youthful rioters. Through it all the robin sings, "Summertime, and the living is easy," and I wish I could sit down and have a heart-to-heart talk with the merry moron. I would tell him that it is easy enough to be light-hearted if you have not got yourself involved in the Broadway theatre. And if that cued him into "Give my regards to Broadway," I should probably make a pass at him with a fly swatter and order him out of the house, or the tree.

Editors, and other busy minds, keep asking me what I

think about the future of the American theatre. If they telephone me in the country to ask this question, I always say, with a sigh of relief, "Then you mean it's still alive!" Naturally, I worry about the fabulous invalid, which has got into a far worse state since the 1920s than I have. In 1928, Philip Barry's *Holiday* opened on Broadway on a Monday night in November, and there were four other openings that night, and twelve in all during the week.

Later the legitimate theatre acquired a slow, wasting ailment. It began to develop the nightmares and matinee-mares that now afflict the drama. Once, last summer, when the robin woke me with his Gershwin tune, I lay there retitling certain plays to fit the temper and trend of the present day, and came up with these: *Abie's Irish Neurosis, The Bitter and Ache Man, Ned Macabre's Daughter, I Dismember Mama, They Slew What They Wanted, Toys in the Psychosomatic, The Glands Menagerie, Destroy Writes Again, The Manic Who Came to Dinner,* and, a title calculated to pop you out of bed and into a cold tub, *Oklahomosexual.*

It seems to me that this year's extensive arguments and debates about the morbid and decadent state of so-called serious modern drama skim the surface like skipping stones because they fail to take into consideration the dying out of humor and comedy, and the consequent process of dehumanization, both on stage and off. There were literally dozens of comedies to lighten the heart and quicken the step between, say, *The First Year* and *Life with Father.* These were comedies of American life, familial and familiar, but they seem like ancient history now, something to be discussed solemnly by a present-day Aristotle. They could be more cogently and amusingly discussed by a new Robert Benchley, but, alas, there isn't any.

The decline of humor and comedy in our time has had a multiplicity of causes, a principal one being the ideological beating they have taken from both the intellectual left and the political right. The latter came about through the intimidation of writers and playwrights under McCarthyism. The former is more complex. Humor has long been a target of leftist intellectuals, and the reason is simple enough in itself. Humor, as Lord Boothby has said, is the only solvent of terror and tension, and terror and tension are among the chief ideological weapons of Communism. The leftists have made a concerted attack on humor as an antisocial, antiracial, antilabor, antiproletarian stereotype, and they have left no stereotype unused in their attack, from "no time for comedy" to the grim warnings that humor is a sickness, a sign of inferiority complex, a shield and not a weapon.

The modern morbid playwrights seem to have fallen for the fake argument that only tragedy is serious and has importance, whereas the truth is that comedy is just as important, and often more serious in its approach to truth, and, what few writers seem to realize or to admit, usually more difficult to write.

It is not a curious but a natural thing that arrogant intellectual critics condemn humor and comedy, for while they can write about Greek Old Comedy, Middle Comedy, and New Comedy with all the flourishes of pretension, they avoid a simple truth, succinctly expressed by the *Oxford*

142

Classical Dictionary in its discussion of Middle Comedy. "Before long the realistic depiction of daily life became the chief aim in Comedy. Ordinary, commonplace life is no easy subject to treat interestingly on the stage; and Antiphanes contrasts the comic poet's more difficult lot with the tragedian's, whose plot is already familiar, and the *deus ex machina* at hand—the comic writer has no such resources."

The history of stage comedy, in both Greece and Rome, begins with cheap and ludicrous effects. In Greek Old Comedy there were the padded costumes of the grotesque comedian, the paunch and the leather phallus. The Roman Plautus, in freely translating Greek New Comedy, stuck in gags to make his rough and restless audiences guffaw, so that in the beginning comedy was, to use a medical term, exogenous—that is, not arising from within the human being, but dragged in from the outside. The true balance of life and art, the saving of the human mind as well as of the theatre, lies in what has long been known as tragicomedy, for humor and pathos, tears and laughter are, in the highest expression of human character and achievement, inseparable. Many dictionaries, including the OED, wrongly hyphenate tragicomedy, as if the two integral parts were warring elements that must be separated.

I think the first play that ever sent me out of the American theatre in a mood of elation and of high hope for our stage was *What Price Glory?* Amidst all the blood and slaughter there ran the recurring sound of congruous laughter. I still vividly remember the scene in which the outraged French father of an outraged daughter babbles

143

his grievance for a full minute to the bewildered Captain Flagg, who then asks a French-speaking American lieutenant, "What did he say?"

"Rape," says the lieutenant.

That scene fairly shines with humanity when compared to an episode in the recent *There Was a Little Girl* in which the raped little girl solemnly asks her seducer if she had enjoyed the experience. And I can still recall the gleams of humor in R. C. Sheriff's *Journey's End*, as bitter a war play as any.

"What kind of soup *is* this, Sergeant?" asks Captain Stanhope.

"Yellow soup, sir," says the mess sergeant, apologetically.

Screen writers, as well as playwrights, seem reluctant, or unable, to use the devices of comedy out of fear of diluting suspense. A few years ago, in a movie about a bank clerk who stole a million dollars, crammed it into a suitcase, got into a taxi with his unaware and bewildered wife, and headed for an airport to flee the country, there came a scene in which he handed the driver a fifty-dollar bill and told him to "Step on it." Now I submit that the wife of an American male of modest income would have gone into a comedy scene at this point, but the writer or writers of the script must have been afraid that such an interlude would ruin the terror and tension, and terror and tension must be preserved nowadays, even at the expense of truth.

Katharine Hepburn recently said that our playwrights should "rise above their time," but, if they tried that, they would simply sink below themselves, or sit there staring at the blank paper in their typewriters. Separate molds turn out unvarying shapes. You can't make a Tennessee Ernie out of a Tennessee Williams, any more than you can turn a callin' back into a trough cleanin'. A callin' back, if you don't know, is a gatherin' of folks at the bedside of a dyin' man, to call him back. I hope this doesn't inspire one of the morbid playmakers to make a play in which the dyin' man drags all the other folks down with him.

It will be said, I suppose, that I couldn't write such a tragedy because of the limitation of my tools and the nature of my outlook. (Writers of comedy have outlook, whereas writers of tragedy have, according to them, insight.) It is true, I confess, that if a male character of my invention started across the stage to disrobe a virgin criminally (ah, euphemism to end euphemisms!), he would probably catch his foot in the piano stool and end up playing "Button Up Your Overcoat" on the black keys. There are more ways than one, including, if you will, a Freudian stumble, to get from tragedy into tragicomedy. Several years ago a book reviewer in the New York Sunday *Times* wrote: "The tragedy of age is not that a man grows old, but that he stays young," and, indeed, there is the basis of a good tragedy in that half-truth. The other half might be stated, in a reverse Shavian paraphrase, "The trouble with youth is that it is wasted on the old." There is where the comedy would come in to form a genuine tragicomedy. At sixty-six, going on sixty-seven, I think I can speak with a touch of authority.

Miss Hepburn (to get back to her) is devoted to the

145

great plays of Shakespeare, who didn't rise above his time, but merely above the ability of his contemporaries. He often wrote about a time worse than his own, such as the period of Macbeth. In that drama he could proclaim that life is a tale told by an idiot, full of sound and fury, signifying nothing, but say it in a play told by a genius, full of soundness and fury, signifying many things. The distinguished Mr. Williams and his contemporaries are not so much expressers of their time as expressions of it, and, for that matter, aren't we all? The playwright of today likes to believe that he is throwing light upon his time, or upon some part of it, when his time is actually throwing light upon him. This, it seems to me, has always been the case, but it happens more intensely now, perhaps, than ever before. Moreover, there are two kinds of light, the glow that illumines and the glare that obscures, and the former seems to be dimming.

The American family, in spite of all its jitters and its loss of cohesion, still remains in most of its manifestations as familiar as ever, and it is our jumpy fancy to believe that all fathers are drunkards, all mothers kookies, and all children knife wielders planning to knock off their parents. Our loss of form in literature is, in large part, the result of an Oral Culture into which we began descending quite a while back. This is the age of the dragged-out interview, the endless discussion panels on television; an age in which photographers, calling on writers in their homes, stay around the house as long as the paper hanger or the roofer. Everything is tending to get longer and longer, and more and more shapeless. Telephone calls last as long as half an hour, or even forty minutes by my own count; women, saying good-by at front doors, linger longer than ever, saying, "Now I *must* go," and, eventually "Now, I *really* must go." But nothing is accomplished simply any more. Writers of letters finish what they have to say on page two and then keep on going. Khrushchev talks for five hours at press conferences, and may even have got it up to ten by the time this survey appears. (Moral: Great oafs from little icons grow.)

As brevity is the soul of wit, form, it seems to me, is the heart of humor and the salvation of comedy. "You are a putter in, and I am a taker out," Scott Fitzgerald once wrote to Thomas Wolfe. Fitzgerald was not a master of comedy, but in his dedication to taking out, he stated the case for form as against flow. It is up to our writers, in this era of Oral Culture, to bring back respect for form and for the innate stature and dignity of comedy. We cannot, to be sure, evoke humorists, or writers of comedy, by prayer or pleading or argument, but we can, and must, hope for a renascence of recognizable American comedy. The trend of the modern temper is toward gloom, resignation, and even surrender, and there is a great wailing of the word "Decadence!" on all sides. But for twenty-five hundred years decadence has come and decadence has gone. Reading Webster on the subject might make a newly arrived visitor from Mars believe that everything in art and literature came to a morose end as the nineteenth century closed out. It was a period of Decadence and of the Decadents, led by Baudelaire, Verlaine, and Mallarmé in France. Writes old Noah: "They cultivated the ab-

147

normal, artificial, and neurotic in subject and treatment, tending to the morbid or eccentric, and to the mystically sensuous and symbolic."

Well, we are still going on, and we have four decades left in this battered and bloody century. Walter Lippmann said last summer, in his first television appearance, that he did not believe the world is coming apart. It is heartening to know that he selected as the foremost leader of our time Sir Winston Churchill, a man also respected for his wit and humor. It is high time that we came of age and realized that, like Emily Dickinson's hope, humor is a feathered thing that perches in the soul.

18

Here Come the Dolphins

How sharper than a sermon's truth it must have been
for many human beings when they learned that bottle-
nosed Dolphin may, in time, succeed battle-poised Man as
the master species on earth. This prophecy is implicit in
the findings of those scientists who have been studying,
and interviewing, dolphins in laboratories. It neither
alarms nor surprises me that Nature, whose patience with
our self-destructive species is giving out, may have decided
to make us, if not extinct, at least a secondary power
among the mammals of this improbable planet.

Clarence Day, in his *This Simian World*, prefigured, in
turn, the tiger and the dog as the master species, if their
evolution, instead of ours, had turned them into People.
He did not think of the dolphin, that member of the

whale family sometimes called, inaccurately, the porpoise or the grampus. As far back as 1933 I observed a school of dolphins (their schools increase as ours decline) romping, as we carelessly call it, alongside a cruise ship in the South Atlantic, and something told me that here was a creature, all gaiety, charm, and intelligence, that might one day come out of the boundless deep and show us how a world can be run by creatures dedicated not to the destruction of their species but to its preservation.

We shall, alas, not be on earth to hear the lectures, and to read the reports, on Man by a disinterested intelligence equal, and perhaps superior, to our own. I should like to hear a thoughtful and brilliant dolphin cutting us down to our true size, in that far day when the much-vaunted Dignity of Man becomes a footnote to history, a phrase lifted from the dusty books of human sociologists and the crumbling speeches of obliterated politicians.

Anyone, even a human being, capable of contemplation and the exercise of logic, must realize that what has been called the neurotic personality of our time is rapidly becoming psychopathic. One has but to look at and listen to those anti-Personality Cultists, Khrushchev and Castro, to identify them as the most notorious personality cultists of our era. I mourn the swift mortality of Man that will prevent him from reading *The Decline and Fall of Man* by Professor B. N. Dolphin. What I am saying will, of course, be called satire or nonsense. Professor Dolphin can deal with that when the time comes.

Almost all of Man's self-praise is exaggerated and magnified by the muddled and conflicting concepts of religion, sociology, and philosophy. We are not, for instance, the most adjustable of creatures, but the most helpless and desperate, so that we have had to develop ingenuity of a high and flexible kind in order to survive. All the other creatures of earth, with the exception of those we have made dependent by domestication, are more adjusted than we are, and can, and must, get along without us. But we depend upon many of them for our existence as we depend upon vegetables. It is impossible to imagine a female seal saying to another female seal "What a charming ladyskin! Where did you get it?" And I have just learned from a doctor friend of mine who spent six months in the Antarctic that the human being down there invariably suffers from Big Eye—that is, the inability to sleep well, or at all. And everybody knows that the penguins adjusted to their climate and that they never develop stomach ulcers since they long ago discovered a wholesome and nurturing diet, which we couldn't do even if we had another million years to live.

The penguin eats plankton, a nourishing if somewhat despondent food, charmingly described by the dictionary as "the passively floating and weakly swimming animal and plant life of a body of water." Man, being Man, doesn't care much for submissive victuals, but loves to beat the hell out of some of his main dishes, and has devised a dozen weapons with which to kill them, on sea or land or in the air, from the fish hook and the harpoon to the rifle and the shotgun. The penguin and the dolphin, beholding the dismaying spectacle of human beings at table, will surely exclaim, when they learn English, "What foods these mortals eat!"

I cannot be there to see, but I can clearly visualize what will happen when dolphinity has replaced humanity as the primary power. I can picture the dolphins' first ambassador to Washington or to the Court of St. James's coming into the presence of the President or the Prime Minister and saying with a wink and a whistle, "Ours is a porpoiseful society. Good-by, and sorry, and may there be a proper moaning of the bar when you, who came from out the boundless deep, return again home."

Oh, but there is still time, gentlemen! Let's uncork the bottles, call up the ladies, exchange with our enemies the well-worn accusations of imperialistic ambitions, and lean back. Let us have our fun before we are officially advised that, as Henley put it, our little job is done. And make mine a double Scotch and soda while you're at it. I have become a touch jittery myself, meditating that human marriage, whose success and failure both have helped to put us where we are, will seem, one fine century in the future, as quaint and incredible to the dolphins as the hipbone of a dinosaur.

19

Conversation
Piece: Connecticut

It was our couple's day off, and since my wife was across the road calling on a neighbor when I got up, I was alone in the house, or thought I was. I had gone out to the refrigerator for my glass of orange juice, and had come back to the living room with it, muttering to myself about something that annoyed me—the inertia of Longstreet at Gettysburg, or the assumption that the concept of eternal bliss is a reward rather than a cruel and unusual punishment of the kind proscribed by the Constitution of the United States, or the tendency of strangers to write to me in longhand, signing their names in a scrawl that looks like "Djimn Hovnbg"—when the voice of a man broke in on my dark thoughts. He was sitting in a chair in a far corner of the living room, and he began in the middle of his own thoughts.

"You seem to be unaware that everybody is crazy," he said, "owing to a fallout of finely powdered fruitcake over the planet. In every office building, in every place where many people gather, there should be a sign reading, 'DANGER! 10,000 DOLTS.'"

"Good morning," I said, sitting on the edge of a chair and sipping my juice.

"I made myself a drink," said my uninvited visitor.

"There's a time for drinking," I told him.

"I am nutty, too, because of the fruitcake," he went on. "All I can think of is nervous ailments. Have you heard of the roofer who got shingles from Sears, Roebuck? Or the steeplechase horse with the galloping jumps, or the jittery cupbearer of the gods who had the Hebe Jeebies, or the three-legged descendant of Lassie afflicted with the collie wobbles?"

"No," I said. "What worries *me* is that 'thing' has developed a past tense, rare in any noun, you must admit. It has become 'thung'—'thing,' 'thang,' 'thung,' as in 'sing,' 'sang,' 'sung.' The way into the past tenses is downhill and gloomy, but fortunately the road goes uphill on the other side of the dark valley, and we climb out of thung into thing again. This is because of the cyclical nature of the species. We all go from thing to thung and back again, depending on our individual cycles. Right now, you seem to be thunger than I am. There is a ring in the very sound of 'thing,' but 'thung' is a fungus. At the low point of the cycle, one's fingers become fungers. Our fingers never actually become all thumbs. That is pure imprecision of definition. During the fungers phase, a surgeon should not be permitted to use a scalpel, jugglers drop what they are juggling, and everyone is a danger to himself and to others."

"You miss the point," said my guest irritably. "The trouble is that we allowed 'think' to become 'thought.' When man developed the tendency to end certain past tenses with the letters 'ught,' he slowed down his own think processes. It was all right when 'drink' became 'drank,' for the word and the act still had bounce, but—"

"What worries you," I said, "is what may yet happen. You are afraid the day will come when a woman, in reporting a winking man to a policeman, will say, 'I want to report a man who wought at me.' "

"What?" asked my strange guest.

"'Wought,'" I repeated.

"*I'll* ask the questions," he said petulantly. "I'll also answer them. If I'm wrong, I'll correct myself."

I made a gesture with my empty glass, indicating that this was my house, not his. "There was no reason for 'fight' to become 'fought,'" I said. "There was a time when a man was knighted for fighting, not knought because he had fought. The great good place, the lighted place, has become the lought place, so close to lost that our last link with light is—"

"You go around in tiny circles," he said, and he crossed to where I keep my liquor and made himself another highball. On his way back to his chair, he picked up a book from an end table and waved it at me. "This book was bought," he said. "Where did you bink it?"

"What makes you think I did bink it?" I demanded. "Maybe what I did was bight it."

"We are both wrong," my visitor said. "There's an inscription in this book, proving that you did not bink it or bight it. It was given to you."

"Logic is too big to apply to little matters, or mutters," I said. "We are getting into insemantics, or the meaninglessness of meaninglessness. There are three monsters one must avoid—the Loch Ness monster, the togetherness monster, and the meaninglessness monster. Any minute now you'll say that the hope of the world, or of the word, lies in turning everything that ends in 'ouse' into 'ice'— in the plural, that is."

"What are you yammering about now?" he demanded.

156

"I am referring to mouse and mice," I said stiffly. "Why, of all the hice in this town, did you have to wander into mine?"

"Not long ago," he began, paying no attention to what I had said, "you wrote, or wrought, an article—it sounded wrought to me—in which you said that 'evening' was a lovely word of two syllables, never three, and then a woman who proudly described herself as disagreeable wrought you a letter in which she maintained that if most people called it 'cat,' then 'evening' would properly *become* 'cat.'"

"I don't know how you know about the lady's letter," I said.

"I know you like a bought book, brother," he said impatiently. "You replied to her letter and then tore up your reply. Yet you made one excellent point. I refer to your bringing up the artillery of music and poetry, harmonics and metre and melody, against those persons—those monsters of mindlessness—who believe that proper English usage should be determined by a majority vote, as in the elections of the late President Harding and Governor Long of Louisiana."

"Thank you," I said. "No, let me mix this one for you." I took his glass and carried it to the bar. "I have the vanity to believe I did get over, in my letter to the lady, one telling thrust. I wrote, 'Sunset and cat star, and one clear scat for you.'"

"Excellent, excellent," he said jovially. "Why didn't you send the letter?"

For answer, I quoted a line from Landor. "'I strove with

none, for none was worth my strife,' " I said.

"Don't brag," he told me. "It is mainly with those not worth our strife that we strive. The chances of winning are better. Why don't you put a record on your Magnavox there? Something instrumental, maybe. Get away from words for a while."

"It's no use," I said. "When I play music, I think of music. I mean the word 'music.' Have you ever tried re-arranging the letters of that word, in an effort to arrive at a group that doesn't make you ill?"

"Why should I?" he asked uneasily. "Life is hard enough when one is feeling well."

"The word is icsum and mucsi," I said. "It is also musci and scumi. If you say 'Sicum!' your dog starts bark-ing at nothing, and if you say 'Sucim,' the pigs in the barnyard begin squealing and grunting. 'Muics' is the cat's miaow. Say 'miscu' and your fingers are fungers, say 'umsci' and the Russians are upon you. As for mucis—my God, are you ready for another drink already?"

"Yes, and make it double," he said. "When you turn words inside out, you turn your stomach upside down—don't you know that?"

"I know all about it," I said, fixing him a stiff one. "I often wish I could let words alone, and not lie in bed re-arranging 'Geneva' to get 'avenge,' or spelling 'repaid' backward, or—"

"Speaking of backward," he said, "you probably know that Red Grange becomes Der Egnarg. And which do you prefer for that Indian movie actress—Das Gupta or Sad Atpug?"

"I don't want any part of either one of them," I said sharply. I snatched his glass from him and took a long slug of the double Scotch just as my wife came into the room.

"Drinking already?" she demanded. "Do you realize it isn't noon yet?"

"I am trying to be a good host," I told her. "This gentleman fixed two drinks for himself, and then I made his next two."

"What gentleman?" she asked blankly.

I stood there a moment, holding my unexpected visitor's glass, and realized that he was no longer there. "He is gone," I said.

"You're the one that's gone," my wife retorted, "or will be if you finish that drink. Four drinks before breakfast! I'll scramble you a couple of eggs and make some coffee right away." She whisked the glass away from me and hurried out into the kitchen.

"You dog," I said to the empty chair in the corner. "You got me into this."

I managed to eat a piece of toast and drink two cups of coffee, but I decided to skip the eggs. My wife shook her head at me. "It wasn't Scotch," I said defensively, "it was music." Then I went back to bed. I lay there for a while thinking of the Sesumarongi, a backward tribe but a tribe that is all around us.

20

How the Kooks
Crumble

I am now convinced that American radio, or what is left of it, is unconsciously intent (I hope it's unconsciously) upon driving such of its listeners as are not already kooky, kooky. Before we proceed with the indictment, let's examine the slang noun "kook," from which the adjective "kooky" is derived. The newest Dictionary of American Slang has this to say about "kook": "n. An odd, eccentric, disliked person; a 'drip'; a nut. Teenage use since 1958; rapidly becoming a pop. fad word. Kooky, adj. crazy, nuts; odd, eccentric; having the attributes of a 'drip.'"

It seems to me that the Dictionary of American Slang is a little odd or eccentric (I don't say crazy or nuts) when it fails to trace "kook" and "kooky" to the much older slang word "cuckoo" or "coo-coo." It might also have pointed out the possibility that the new word derives from Kukla of the old Kukla, Fran, and Ollie television program. According to the slang dictionary, the female European cuckoo is the bird that lays its eggs in another bird's nest, which may be odd or eccentric, but, as any mother will tell you, is by no means crazy or nuts. The American female cuckoo, by the way, hatches its own eggs in its own nest—but let's not get so deeply into this that we can't get out.

My indictment of radio, to return to that, is aimed specifically at most of the news reporters, or reporters of bad news, to be exact. These men seem to revel in news items of horror, terror, catastrophe, and calamity. I have forced myself to listen, during the past few months, to an assortment of these voices of doom which are heard all day long, on the hour or half-hour, over almost all radio stations. It is something in the nature of a God's blessing to cut them off and turn to the intelligent programs on WNYC, and the music of WQXR. It is wonderful to get away from the yelling and howling of what might be called the present-day Creepy Time melodies and lyrics (and I apologize to both of those fine words). One of these gibberings poses the question "What is love?" and answers it with "Five feet of heaven in a pony tail."

But let's get back to those reporters of disaster and death. Most of them seem to have been taught diction, phrasing, and monotone in two separate schools for announcers. One group of these men presents the horror óf fires, automobile accidents, and multiple family murders in a tone of incongruous and chilling, matter-of-fact calm.

The other group leaps upon items of daily terror in a mindless tone of almost eager elation. Let us glance, for as long as we can stand it, at the formula of one of these broadcasts of daily American hell. This kind of program usually lasts fifteen minutes, begins on a high note of cataclysm, and ends with a report of "stocks and the weather." In between, there are often as many as five or six commercials, and in many instances these are read by the reporters themselves in exactly the same tone as the calamities, thus giving the listener the spooky feeling that the deaths of scores of persons in an air crash are no more important than a new candy bar or brand of coffee. But let me set down a mild paraphrase of the broadcasts I am indicting:

"Thirty-seven persons were killed today, and more than one hundred others critically injured, in a chain collision of some twenty-five pleasure cars and trucks on a fog-bound New Jersey highway. Mrs. Marcia Kook, who yesterday shot down eleven members of her family with two double-barreled shotguns, was killed today by her estranged husband, who also took the lives of the couple next door, a mortician out walking his dog, two school-teachers and a nun. Police say that they found two million dollars' worth of heroin fastened to her underclothing. Do you know the true glory of gracious modern living? You don't unless you have tried Becker's Butternut Coffee with that serene, heavenly flavor that you have never tasted before. Try it today and you will try it always. Arthur Kookman, sought by the police of Long Island for having blown up two churches and a nurses' home, was arrested today on a charge of filing a false income tax return. While being arraigned in court, he fired two shots at the judge, one of them killing Sergeant Jeremiah Kookberg in whose apartment police later found seventy-six shotguns, thirty-seven vacuum cleaners, forty-two washing machines, one hundred and fifty refrigerators and three million dollars' worth of heroin. You will think you're in heaven when you taste Tiddly-Bits, the wonderful new chocolate-covered candy mints, as sweet as an angel's kiss."

My long Spooky Time session with the babble box in my living room revealed still another source of what appears to me to be a desire, or compulsion, to drive the nation crazy. This is radio's apparently incurable addiction to frightening statistics. Many of these grow out of a basically worthy attempt to interest listeners in contributing money to various campaigns on behalf of research in heart disease, cancer, muscular dystrophy, and the like. Whoever writes most of these appeals seems invariably constrained to say something like this: "Every eleven seconds in America some man, woman, or child is stricken with Googleman's disease" or "There are more than eleven million people in the United States who suffer from unilateral mentalitis or allied ailments." Among the statistics that I gathered in the course of one afternoon were these consoling figures: there are nineteen million accidents every year in our nation; more than fourteen million Americans have, or have had, some serious mental derangement; fifty-two million dollars' worth of merchandise, comprising all forms of food, is stolen every year from American supermarkets.

It may be that radio, in flooding the daytime and night-time air with horrible news and distressing statistics, banks on the well-established psychological truth that a person is not so much shocked by what happens to somebody else as relieved by the realization that he is, at least for the time being, unstricken and undead. The vast accumulation of all this twisted relief, however, is bound to take its toll of the American mass mind. One afternoon I was joined in front of my radio by three friends who had expressed doubt that so much hell and horror was calmly, or blithely, broadcast to the people of this jumpy republic. They ended up with the admission that I was by no means exaggerating, but even playing the situation down a bit. "Well," said one of them, with a heavy sigh, "*we* are still here." To which another replied, "As the fellow said at the Alamo."

There is, believe it or not, good news about the United States of America easily available to every radio press department if the gloomy gentlemen would care to look for it. Medical research, for instance, is continually turning up new devices and techniques for the cure, or alleviation, of almost all ailments. These are usually reported only in medical journals, but, alas, they do not have the impact of death, derangement, and disaster. I do not, of course, recommend sweetness and light or censorship, but merely the application of that now most uncommon of human qualities, common sense. Recent statistics that I have heard over the air, announced calmly by one school of reporters and gleefully by the other, asserted that a careful examination of some thousands of Americans proved that only eighteen per cent of them were mentally well. Just think of it, folks—if there were a hundred guests at the New Year's Eve party you attended, only eighty-two of them were kooky, cuckoo, crazy, or nuts. Incidentally, the prevalent use of the word "disturbed" to take in all forms and degrees of mental aberration serves only to intensify the encircling gloom. For example, if one says, "She is disturbed by her husband's drinking," it implies that the wife has been driven crazy by it.

Not long ago a woman who was trapped in a New York subway fire, but managed to fight her way to safety, said, "It was wonderful to see people and light." An excellent combination, people and light. We ought to try to bring them together more often.

21

The Watchers of
the Night

Most of the people I like, or love, or can barely stand
are between the ages of forty-five and sixty-five, give or
take a year or two at either end, and only about three of
them are capable any longer of achieving what was once
casually called, and is now wistfully called, a good night's
rest. For ours is the age of the four "A"s: anxiety, apprehension, agonizing, and aspirin. People are smoking more
and enjoying it less, drinking more and feeling it more,
and waking around three in the morning to lie there
gloomily staring at the mushroom-shaped ceiling, listening for the approaching drone of enemy bombers, and
thinking of death but dressing it in the raiment of lyric
or metaphor: the gate in the garden wall, the putting out
to sea, the mother of beauty, the fog in the throat, the

ruffian on the stair, the man in the white coat, the sleep that rounds our little lives.

If a husband wakes at three o'clock in the morning— once fondly known as the hour of a melody that Scott Fitzgerald called sweetly sad—he is not going to be able to lie there agonizing alone, the way his wife can, and frequently does. If they are in New York, which has an average of twelve dozen fire alarms every twenty-four hours, the wakeful husband will hear, sooner or later, the screaming of fire-engine sirens, which do not sound like heroic robots courageously rushing to a scene of disaster but like panicky monsters fleeing from this our life, shrieking hysterically in abject fear. It is at this moment in the dead of night that Papa usually feigns a nightmare in order to wake Mama and enjoy her warm scorn and her comforting scolding for interrupting her sleep. He will now be able to drop off again in a few minutes, but she will lie there, stark-staring awake, long enough to finish one or two mystery novels or to write, in her head, anywhere from five to fifteen letters of objection, correction, criticism, rebuttal, or denial, none of which she ever actually gets down on paper. All this has led to the sale and use of something like sixty-five million tranquillizing pills every year in this jumpy nation of ours.

I have joined the fifteen million people in the United States who are sixty-five years old or older, and for a good, or bad, five years I have been a three-o'clock waker. I dread, as much as anyone else, the white watches of the woeful night, but, unlike most of my insomniac friends and enemies, I often think of the thousands of others who are also lying awake, and during the day I sometimes ask a few of them what they think about when they can't get back to sleep. One man, an architect and artist, says he starts with the town of Azusa, California, and moves eastward, a town and a letter of the alphabet at a time, hoping to doze off before he reaches Zanesville, Ohio. Another man, an overworked literary agent, makes up imaginary baseball teams, and is just now nocturnally engaged in forming one out of players whose names are the same as the names of occupations—Baker, Chandler, Tinker, and the like. No woman, of course, allows herself to fall into such a strange system of seeking sleep, for she is wise enough to know that a practice of that kind is a stimulant and not a soporific.

Since I have no mental discipline to speak of when I am horizontal, and little enough when I am upright, my conscious mind leads me into all kinds of sleep-murdering snarls. The other night, for example, I began with "We supply watchmen to watch men you want watched," and slowly built it up like this: "We supply watchwatchmen to watch watchmen watching men you want watched. We supply watchwomen to watch watchwatchmen watching watchmen watching men you want watched. We supply wristwatches for witchwatchers watching witches Washington wishes watched." At this point I woke Mama, and was asleep again by three-forty-five, while she lay awake long enough to reread *Trent's Last Case* and *The Murder of Roger Ackroyd*. For years now, I have kept myself awake while courting unconsciousness by tinkering with words and letters of the alphabet and spelling words back-

ward. I am not going to spell anything backward in this piece except "ping-pong" and one other expression we shall come to later. "Ping-pong," a trade name for table tennis, was presumably selected for its supposed onomatopoeic effect, but I submit that "gnip-gnop" is much more successful, that it really sounds like a game in progress. Another system of mine, which truly straight-arms sleep, is to rewrite, or paraphrase, Poe's "The Raven" from the viewpoint of the bird instead of that of the man.

Once upon a daybreak dreary,
While I fluttered sleek and cheery
Over many a granule of ungarnered corn,
Suddenly there came a moaning, as of someone loudly
  groaning,
Groaning at the thought of morn.

This version ends up with the raven trapped on the pallid
bust of Pallas just above the chamber door. In other
words, the unfortunate bird, lured into the sleepless
scholar's chamber, has become a room raven. It was but
the mental work of half an hour to figure—nay, to prove—
that the raven speaks English with a foreign accent, and
you can find this out for yourself simply by spelling "room
raven" backward, beginning with the second word. This,
to be sure, gets neither me nor you (nor Poe and the
raven) anywhere except into the bad habit of mental left-
reading in bed at night, and I guess I'm sorry I brought
it up. (If Poe had rewritten "The Raven" in order to
retract something, the result would have been a palinode,
I thought you might want to know.)

One noon recently, I woke up, weak and weary, having
spent the time between three o'clock and five o'clock in
the morning trying to figure out all the possible reasons
for what the psychiatrists call leucophobia, an irrational
fear of white or whiteness. I couldn't find the word in any
dictionary I own—I had picked it up in a conversation
with a psychologist I know—and so I telephoned him and
asked him to explain the origin of this peculiar phobia, for
the normal mind, if any, finds it puzzling that the raiment
of the bride, the color of the Cliffs of Dover, the symbol

of snow and sleigh bells at Christmastime should be a source of terror. The explanation, insofar as anyone knows, is that the fear is rooted in that most ancient of superstitions, the notion that ghosts are always clad in white and that death itself is therefore white. "The Ku Klux Klan," said my psychologist friend, "unquestionably adopted robes and hoods of white to perpetuate in their victims the terror of the ghost." The next morning, at three o'clock, the waking hour, the ghostly hour, I began searching for other possible sources of fear in that innocent conjunction of all colors. I thought of the white radiance of eternity, the white plague, the White Lady, white heat, white cargo, white rage, white water (the sign of the surfacing whale), and the White House and the Great White Father, which and who, respectively, have terrified, during one Presidential administration and another, not only the red man but also the paleface and, many would like to believe, the yellow man. Then there are the white corpuscles, whose increase can be fatal; the whited sepulchre; and the Great White Way (a term often credited to Albert Bigelow Paine, biographer of that great and far from fearsome man who loved to dress all in white, Mark Twain). We also have, in our culture or history or folklore, the whites of their eyes, white lies that can be so dangerous, the white feather of cowardice, the white flag of surrender—but you can take it from there; if you are a three-clock waker, it will ensure your staying awake until the first white light of dawn.

For those watchers of the night who wake at the old Scott Fitzgerald hour and know darn well they are not going to get to sleep again, I suggest a ramble, a fascinating safari, through one of the letters of the alphabet. (It just occurred to me that some of my readers may think I didn't list above the White Rabbit of Wonderland because I am afraid of the White Rabbit, but I am not afraid of any white animal except the white elephant, which is always, in some form or other, on my hands day and night.) I have for weeks now been exploring the sixteenth letter of the alphabet, and have had more fun than a barrel of money (a barrel of monkeys is never fun but often, I should imagine, sheer hell, especially for the monkeys at the bottom of the barrel).

The letter "P," that broad, provocative expanse between "O" and "Q," is one of the most ambivalent of all the twenty-six, for in it one finds pleasure and pain, peace and pandemonium, prosperity and poverty, power and pusillanimity, plethora and paucity, pornography and prudery, purity and prurience, public and private, pastime and punishment, the patrician and the proletarian, and on and on, words without end.

Wanderers in the wide verbal terrain between "O" and "Q," with its panorama of plain and prairie, plateau and palisade, peninsula and promontory, can get on their horses and ride off in any one of all directions. It is well known, thanks to Clarence Day, that it is the wife, it is the home, that will not let the sailor roam and keeps the pioneer in town. This being the case, the wakeful captive husband is likely to see how far he can get from home and Mama, in fancy and fantasy. I play a night game called place-to-place, or around-the-world-in-eighty-names. The goal, a hopeless one, is to recall fourscore place names that strike no alarm bells in the memory. I hear none in Punxsutawney, or Papeete, or Irvin Cobb's Paducah, but from there on man and nature have made the going rough, with Pakistan, Peiping, Panama, Pompeii, Pelée—and there are still seventy-two more to come. It isn't easy to think only of Picardy's shining roses, or of the poppies of Provence, for both places are stained with blood as well as blossoms. The nocturnal wanderer, if he really wants to get his mind off himself and his era, might combine places and pastimes, and linger peacefully, for a little while, anyway, playing parcheesi in Put-in-Bay, post office in Perth Amboy, pinochle in Point Pleasant, polo in Paraguay, poker near Popocatepetl, pedro in Peru, and pigs-in-clover in Port Chester, but the chances of dozing off while wrestling with these imaginary dualities are slim. You are likely to get in deeper and deeper, until you are playing pillow with a pretty poetess in Patchen Place, or pitching pennies with the Pittsburgh Pirates in a pitter-patter of rain outside the Pitti Palace. (Select your own town for prisoner's base, pussy-wants-a-corner, and philopena—a playful practice, also known as "forfeits," which the Germans call *Vielliebchen,* or sweetheart.)

The experienced souse will not linger long in a letter that serves little more than punch, porter, Pernod, pop, Pepsi, Dr. Pepper, Pilsner, Peruna, pousse-café, and—but our souse has already staggered on to the stronger drinks of "R" and "S" and "W," waving aside the philtre that makes a person philous, for sex is not his weakness, and for him Philomela plays her lyre of gold in vain. But,

174

being a man who lives, or at least lies awake, dangerously, I plunge into the phlora and phauna, many of which are nature's caricatures (like pygmies and other people): the platypus in the pansies, the peacock in the pennyroyal, the python in the philodendron, the porcupine in the peonies, and the potto in the potted palms (the poodle, if you must know, is in the pantry among the patisserie, or prone in the parlor or on the porch). Above me, while I watch and wander in this wondrous wilderness, fly the pelican, puffin, ptarmigan, parrot, parakeet, and, a split second before I wake Mama, the pterodactyl.

The person who really wants to get back to sleep should visualize falling snow, floating flowers, the drowsy descent of apple or cherry blossoms, the thin white line upon the shore, being careful that the face of no one particular Sylvia drifts through his waking dreams. Counting sheep is both passé and perilous, for it leads to moondoggling— that is, counting the pugs and Pekes and Poms in lunar rockets. What has kept me awake most recently are the wonderful pixies of "P," major and minor, immortal and ephemeral—and, my God, are they plentiful: Puck, Punch, Punchinello, Pinocchio, Pan, Peter Pan, the Pied Piper, Peter Piper, Prunella, Pierrot and Pierrette, Prancer, Pogo, Penrod, Mary Poppins, Joe Palooka, the Pimpernel, Prospero, Pollyanna, Peg o' My Heart, Puss in Boots, Pooh, the Pod (out of *Sybil's Garden of Pleasant Beasts,* and if you have a copy you're lucky), Popeye (the sailor-man, not the Faulkner fiend), Peck (the naughty son of old man Peck, not Gregory), Pluto (Disney's dizzy dog), and Paddock (the frog friend of the witches in *Macbeth*).

175

There are some wonderfully pixillated people in Bulfinch and in the Oxford Classical Dictionary: Pandora, the bungling busy-fingers who let all hell out of her hope chest; Proteus, the quick-change artist, who had more semblances than Ed Wynn had hats; and Phaëthon, patron saint of the hot-rodsters of today, who drove the chariot of the sun wildly through the skies. Then there was my special pet, Phryne, a courtesan who lived in the fourth century B.C. Once, "she laid aside her garments, let down her hair, and stepped into the sea in the sight of the people." On another occasion, she was brought to trial on a charge of having profaned the Eleusinian mysteries. Things looked pretty bad for her until her counsel "rent her robe and displayed her bosom, which so moved her judges that they acquitted her." Our sixteenth letter played a prominent part in her life—a statue of her was made by Praxiteles, her story was told by Pliny, and it was during the festival of Poseidon that she stepped naked into the sea.

The marvelous sixteenth letter of the alphabet is, to be sure, the country of predicament, plight, problem, perplexity, pickle, pretty pass, puzzle, pit, pitfall, and palindrome. There are many nighttime palindromists in America, caught, or hooked, by the lure of searching for words or phrases that are spelled the same way forward and backward. Among the oldest are "Madam I'm Adam," and "lewd did I live, & evil I did dwel," which are child's play compared to such a new beauty as "a man, a plan, a canal, Panama." I am in touch with several palindrome addicts who have come up with things like "deified," "he

176

goddam mad dog, eh?," and a few longer flights in which slight misspellings are permissible—one of them being the ten-word boast of a queen who drank beer after rum and still managed a good night's rest: "Piel's lager on red rum did murder no regal sleep."

There is one pre-eminent category of "P" that lifts the heart, inspires the spirit, and fortifies faith in man, even if you don't get back to sleep, and that is the category of the pioneers, the pilgrims, and the pathfinders, the immortal heroes of the Shining Quests: Sir Percivale and the Holy Grail; Sir Palamedes and the Questing Beast; Perseus and the dread Medusa; Peary and the North Pole; Ponce and the Fountain of Youth; Marco Polo and the trade routes to the East; Pickett, who tried to reach Washington through the center of Meade's line; Pollux, who helped find the Golden Fleece; Porthos, one of the picaresque posse that set out in pursuit of the queen's diamonds; the brothers Piccard, who hunted for everything, in balloons and bathyspheres; and I almost forgot Plato, who searched for truth (Pontius Pilate just asked what it was, and doesn't belong here), and Pythagoras, who sought to trace the flight of the human soul.

I have some special fictional favorites, including the prince who traced the glass slipper; old Pew, who tracked down Captain Billy Bones and passed him the black spot; Prothero, of *The Research Magnificent;* Hercule Poirot; Lord Peter; Mr. Pinkerton; Colonel Primrose; old Philo; Saul Panzer; and Paladin; and there must be many more. Almost forty years ago, a colleague of mine invented an ephemeral comic detective, and it could only have been the powerful pull of the letter "P" that made him call his sleuth Ploermell. The same pull has operated through centuries of literature and has led to the naming of such comics, or drolls, or grotesques as Pantagruel, Pickwick, Pecksniff, Peggotty, Mr. Pim, Mr. Polly, Prufrock, the Paycock, Pooh-Bah, Sancho Panza, and Henry James's Pocock, just to skim the surface. As for the lure of alliteration, from *Piers Plowman* through *Pride and Prejudice* and *The Pit and the Pendulum* to *Peyton Place* there are hundreds, if you want to lie there hunting titles.

The nocturnal wanderer in the prolific consonant should avoid the area of disease, both physical and mental, if he doesn't want to scare himself to death. "P" seems to be afflicted with almost all of the major ailments and maladies of mind and body, so it's fortunate that it also has the physician, psychologist, psychiatrist, pharmacist, pathologist, and literally dozens of their colleagues, as well as the pope, preacher, parson, priest, prelate, primate, padre, and a helpful host of others.

Let us glance at some of the reasons for the presence of these people, at the risk of becoming a touch scholarly but, I hope, not stuffy. In the Old English or Anglo-Saxon vocabulary, the fewest words began with "P." It had only half as many as the letter "I" and even fewer than "Y." Then, as man prattled on, the letter became the third largest in the alphabet, with only "S" and "C" exceeding its output. The triad formed by these three letters now gives our vocabulary one-third of all its words. The accessions were Germanic and Teutonic, to begin with, and then it began receiving the rich heritage of French and the other Romance languages, and Greek and Latin, especially words beginning with Latin prefixes. There were other additions, too, as time went on, from what the indispensable Oxford English Dictionary calls "the Oriental, African, American, and other remote languages." Furthermore, many additions of words beginning with "P" are of unknown origin, which causes the O.E.D. to observe, "P thus presents probably a greater number of unsolved etymological problems than any other letter."

One phenomenon of "P" that puzzles me is that it rarely starts any word of the dozens that embrace meteorological disturbance, or the antic activities and displays of the elements and the universe that often terrified prehistoric man. Let us list a few of them: weather, heat, cold, rain, blow, snow, hail, sleet, slush, frost, freeze, lightning, thunder, cloudburst, storm, tempest, torrent, flood, fire, hurricane, cyclone, tornado, twister, typhoon, monsoon, simoom, mistral, williwaw, fog, waterspout, eclipse, comet, meteor, meteorite, shooting star, aurora borealis or northern lights, blizzard, gale, earthquake, temblor, tidal wave, avalanche, and landslide. Even counting its internal appearances, "P" shows up only four times in this long list, or no oftener than in the eleven letters of "Pippa Passes." The trouble is, of course, that the would-be sleeper, supine or prone or sidewise, has to get drenched, frozen, sunburned, struck by lightning, and tossed around before he discovers this unique tranquillity in the strange sixteenth letter. Incidentally, "P," when entered in a ship log, means, of all things a skipper encounters at sea, "passing showers."

I suggest that a married couple, in one bed or twin beds, sedulously avoid playing the letter game together in the middle of the night. Mama is sure to get sore because her spouse has ignored Lily Pons, Mary Pickford, Patti Page, Portia, Mrs. Pankhurst, Mrs. Potter Palmer, Pocahontas, Molly Pitcher, and all the other great ladies of the letter, and she is more than likely to defend Pandora as not being a pixie at all, but a lady more important than Prometheus, who started a lot of trouble by bringing fire to our poor planet. Papa will claim that Pandora was a mischievous cutup, comparable to the poltergeist, and far less interesting than the porpoise, that chuckling prankster of the sea, or the penguin, the playbird of the polar parts. The argument, as you can perceive, is capable of going on until cockcrow.

"P," the purloining letter, the stealer of sleep, is as hard to throw off as any addiction. The wanderer, free of its mazes, finds himself returning, remembering the Plantagenet of the Lion Heart, who sought to wrest the Holy Sepulchre from the infidels; Porgy, of the hapless hunt for Bess; and Pershing, who pursued Pancho. I left the sticky letter behind at five o'clock on the morning of this report, only to find myself looking up "white" in the O.E.D. It didn't surprise me much to learn that it once had many pleasant meanings that long ago became obsolete: propitious, favorable, auspicious, fortunate, happy, highly prized, precious, dear, beloved, favorite, pet, darling, fair-seeming, plausible.

The tireless researchers of the O.E.D. staff haven't missed much in the long and far from simple annals of "white," and, in the thirteenth and supplemental volume, they finally got around to "white mule" for gin, but they make no mention of "white" for alcohol, as in "a gallon of white," used by bootleggers during prohibition. It may be a truth of languages that the happy connotations of words tend to die out, and disturbing ones to increase. "White wings" once romantically meant the sails of ships, but it now brings street-cleaners to mind. And, alas, the white rose no longer speaks of love but of tea. Since the good references diminish, I was sorry to hear, one night on television, Jonah Jones change the color of the "little white light" in "My Blue Heaven" to red.

Prisoners of parody and paraphrase, prostrate and pillowed, are prone to tinker with the world and words of Lewis Carroll at the slightest prod or provocation. And so my very latest nights have been plagued by persistent poppycockalorum like this: "'Twas throllog and the siren tones did shriek and gibber in the night, all menace were the bomberdrones, and the mom wrath outright." But enough of this, and, if you should ever be able to fall asleep at night from now on, pleasant dreams.

22

My Senegalese
Birds and Siamese
Cats

I have been going through some yellowing recollections and old dusty whereabouts of mine, with the vague idea of setting down my memoirs now that I am past sixty, and it comes to me with no special surprise that none of them is stained with blood or bright with danger, in the active, or Hemingway, sense of the word. My experiences, like those of most sedentary men fond of creature comforts such as steam heat and room service, have been distinguished by an average unremarkableness, touched with grotesquerie, discomfort and humiliation, but definitely lacking in genuine .50-caliber peril. I have never "met the tiger face to face," as Kipling once put it, or climbed anything higher and colder than half a dozen flights of stairs, or struggled all afternoon to land a fish that outweighed me by three hundred pounds. It occurs to me, however, that some of the most memorable adventures of any man's life are those that have had to be endured in a mood of quiet desperation. I am reminded, for specific example, of a quietly desperate night I spent more than twenty-five years ago on the Blue Train running from Paris to Nice.

After my wife and I had become comfortably ensconced in our sleeping quarters on the train (you can't become ensconced any other way, come to think of it) we discovered, to our dismay, that our Couchette, or Sleepette, or whatever it was called, was to be shared by a short, middle-aged Frenchman, who scowled all the time, occasionally muttered to himself, and didn't even look at us. My wife had bought, in a Paris flower market, God knows why, two Senegalese love-birds which hated each other's guts, and she had insisted on bringing them along. Before we all retired, practically at the same moment—and don't ask me how we managed it—our unexpected companion had kept glancing nervously at the bird cage, which my wife had suspended from something. We had had the two birds for about three weeks and the male had never burst into song, although we had been told that he would. We had gradually come to the conclusion that he couldn't stand his mate, had had no say in her selection, and did not intend to serenade her, or even admit that she was there. They would sit side by side all day long on their little wooden swing, not swinging or ruffling a feather, or even looking at each other, just staring into some happier past. In our hotel room in Paris they had slept all night long, motionless and indifferent to each other, and to us. On the train to Nice they decided, out of some atavistic impulse, to fan out their wings all night long, with intervals of only a few seconds between their rufflings. In such cramped lodgings, about eight by five, the noise they made was the noise of half a dozen Pullman porters busy with

whisk brooms. I can still hear clearly their continual *flut, flut, flut*. It began to get me, it began to get my wife, and it began to get the Frenchman.

Our roommate had gone to bed, composed himself on his back, and pulled on a pair of black cotton gloves. He had then closed his eyes and gone quietly to sleep in a facile way that we envied. He wasn't to sleep long, however, for the flutting began about fifteen minutes after the light had been turned out. The male would flut, and then the female would flut, and then they would flut together. For birds who had never flutted a single flut in three weeks, they turned out to be surprisingly good at it, deeply interested in it, and utterly tireless. After about twenty minutes of the flutting, the Frenchman snarled, "It is necessary to cover those birds." My wife, who spoke excellent French, told him that the birds had been covered, and he suggested that she put something else over their cage. This, she explained to him after groping for the word, would cause them to suffocate. The Frenchman said something in a threatening tone that I didn't get, but which was later translated by my wife as, "It is as well to suffocate as to be strangled." I got up and put my coat over the cage, but the flutting came through as clearly as ever. All night long the three of us would doze off, wake up, and doze off again. Each time the Frenchman woke up he had a different expression, and he ran through everything from "*zut alors*" to what might be roughly translated as, "If a merciful Providence does not silence those birds, I shall throw them off the train and myself after them." (My wife assured me in a whisper that he had said "myself" and not "you.")

Two weeks after we got to our hotel in Nice, we were awakened at dawn one morning by the sound of a bird singing. The sound came, astonishingly enough, from our bird cage, and the song was loud, gay, and full-throated. We got out of bed to explore this incredible phenomenon and discovered that the female was lying dead on the floor of the cage. Whether she had died of boredom, or heartbreak, or had been slain by her hitherto mute "mate," we never, of course, found out. A few days later, we decided to give the male away, cage and all, to an old woman who was selling birds in the flower market of the old town. She was suspicious at first of two Americans who had only one lovebird and who wanted to get rid of it for nothing. "Does he sing?" she asked us doubtfully. My wife didn't have an answer ready for that, but I did. "He sings," I told her, "at funerals." This was literally true. I had decided to bury the dead bird in the garden of the hotel, but I had not known how to get it out to the garden without arousing the suspicion of the French proprietress, a suspicion than which there is none stronger or more durable in the world. Finally, in a kind of elaborate panic, which is customary with me, I had put the unfortunate creature in my pocket and had taken along the cage with the other bird in it. "What in the name of God for?" my wife had asked me, reasonably. "To divert suspicion," I told her. "I will say I am taking him out for an airing. You come too." To this she replied firmly, "No." I managed to bury the dead bird—it was night and the garden was deserted—without attracting onlookers, although I recall that the proprietress seemed relieved later on when we finally checked out of the hotel. The bird in the cage had sung at the funeral not a dirge but an unmistakable roundelay or madrigal, probably a Senegalese version of "She is gone, let her go, God bless her."

The old woman at the flower market stared at me coldly when I mentioned funerals. Experience had doubtless taught her that the line is thinly drawn between American comedy and American insanity. My wife turned away to examine some flowers, with the air of a woman who has become disillusioned and is planning to vanish. I made the mistake, as I always do, of elaborating, and my elaboration in French is something to hear. I think I used the phrase *"goutte de tristesse,"* which literally means "drop of sorrow" and had, as you can see, only the faintest bearing on the situation. Thinking I might be arrested if she allowed me to proceed in my reckless French, my wife rejoined us and came out with the true story of the short unhappy life of the diminutive parrots, ending with a brief account of the mysterious death of one of them. The old woman's eyes lighted with understanding, and she pointed out that the other bird had probably been a male too. This, she added, took the case out of the realm of *crime passionel* and into the realm of *sang-froid*. Since the case was plainly not going to be taken to court, the theory, however sound, seemed immaterial and academic. My wife suddenly broke the silence by demanding twenty-five francs for the survivor. This put the old woman on familiar ground. We began to haggle and compromise. She agreed, in the end, to take the bird for nothing, but her tone was aggrieved. She wanted us to know that she had come off badly, for, as she pointed out, where in the world would she get a Senegalese lovebird as a companion for this solitary male?

Lovebirds, now out of style, and parakeets, now all the rage, belong to the parrot family, but are cousins and not siblings. Lovebirds are found in Africa and South America, and parakeets come from Asia, Africa, Australia and Polynesia. Webster's Unabridged says that lovebirds are "largely green or delicate gray," and their name derives from their habit of perching shoulder to shoulder or, as in the case of my own two, cold shoulder to cold shoulder. Senegal is in French West Africa, an area in which Webster obviously never hunted for small parrots, for he makes no reference to the blue Senegalese lovebird. Mine were blue, all right, and if my memory serves after all this time, each of them had a narrow red ring around its neck, but one ring was narrower and fainter in color than the other, and I had figured this was the mark of the female. I was probably wrong. I don't know any more about lovebirds now than I did then, but my knowledge of females has increased somewhat, and I doubt that I could be fooled again. To be sure, I can be fooled about a female's motives, moods or intentions, and by her fast ball, change of pace and cross fire, but not by the mere fact of her sex.

It was on a later trip to France that my wife bought two female Siamese cats, at the same Paris flower market, the one near the Madeleine. She had come upon the cats one pearly morning in April and couldn't resist buying them and bringing them back to our hotel. Siamese cats, with their unearthly color scheme and their medieval grace, are as handsome as Florentine daggers or exotic jungle orchids, and Circe and Jezzie—short, of course, for Jezebel—were no exception. Now I am not a cat man, but a dog man, and all felines can tell this at a glance—a sharp, vindictive glance. I was all for taking the Siamese cats back to the flower market and, after a good look at me, they were all for going. We were sailing back to New York in a week and I said I had heard somewhere that Siamese cats, like some wines and certain poisons, do not travel well. I went on to invent the theory that this strange Asiatic breed is fragile, possessed of a curious death wish, and inclined to die of seasickness. But when women or children buy cats, they keep cats. If you ever see a Siamese cat thumbing a ride by the side of a lonely road, you can be sure it was surreptitiously put out of a car by a dog man and not by a cat woman. Incidentally, for the guidance of such dog husbands as may have cat wives, it is practically impossible to lose a cat. I have records of cats that have been abandoned as far as 585 miles from home and have managed to find their way back, through traffic and across streams, and against all other odds.

Circe and Jezzie did not enjoy the sea voyage, but they survived it, although there were moments when they seemed to be planning to throw themselves overboard, with the idea in mind, I am sure, of returning to earth later in the guise of spirochetes, or loose cellar steps, or United States Senators with voluminous, unevaluated rumors about my un-Siamese activities. The relations between me and the two female felines deteriorated, gradually but surely, all the way from the Hotel Grand Condé on the Rue Saint Sulpice to my home in Silvermine, Connecticut. My friends began to notice the tension between me and the cats, which consisted largely of rigid immobility on the part of all three of us, and a habit of trying to outstare one another.

"You don't understand cats," one of my friends, Dick Conway, a notorious cat man, told me during a tense weekend at my house. Dick was a writer who found it convenient to explain human and cat problems in terms of eloquent but bewildering metaphors. "You keep showing them your badge," he would tell me. "You pull open a drawer looking for a pistol, not catnip. Siamese cats are full of bells, each with its own sensitive frequency, highly modulated, too, but you insist on tuning in the alarm and not the tinkle."

I would sit back and try to make sense out of this cipher code while Dick and the cats observed me closely. All three of them had eyes of the same shade of blue, six little blue gun barrels trained on me. I tried, somewhat hysterically, I must confess, to maintain a foothold on Dick's idiom. "I do not propose to approach these pets," I said once, "as if I were going to translate them from the Sanskrit." Dick cut in quickly with, "There you go again! You unconsciously put the word 'pets' in quotation marks, and the cats know it. They sense the sardonic instantly."

This was too much for me. "All right, I'll talk to them in upper case from now on!" I yelled. "Or would that sound too much like italics? Italics are smug and pretentious, and I suppose they know that." Dick italicized his superior smile. "Of course they know it," he said quietly. I looked at them and they looked at me. They knew it, all right.

I think that Circe and her confederate—Circe had the darker mask and the blacker silence and the steadier gaze —planned at first to put an end to my life and dispose of my body. What they plotted was a fatal sprawling fall ending in grotesque stillness. One evening I almost stepped on a curiously shaped blue vase the cats had placed on the next to the top step of the stairs going up from the living room, or, as they must have thought of it, coming down from the second floor. A few inches to the left and my foot would have caught the side of the vase, and I would have plunged all the way down the steps. The cats were nowhere around at the time, of course, for the purposes of alibi. I took the vase to my wife, who was in the kitchen, and explained what had almost happened.

"The darlings couldn't possibly lift a thing like that," she said. "You must have put it there yourself. You know how you absently pick up things when you are thinking and put them down where they don't belong." It is true that I had once put a skillet on top of a phonograph, while trying to straighten out a paragraph in my mind, and a loaf of bread I had bought at the grocery turned up, on another occasion, in my bathroom, but the cats were aware of this and their cunning minds had figured out that I would have been held responsible for my own demise if their vase trick had worked. "I hope you won't tell anybody about this," my wife said in conclusion. "They would think something is the matter." Wives have various ways of saying "Something is the matter," and she gave it the inflection that implies the trouble is mental. I decided to tell about the plot anyway at the next party we attended, but I simply didn't know how to begin. If a woman companion says over cocktails, "Have you seen the movies of any good books recently?" you can't very well reply, "No, but my wife's Siamese cats are trying to kill me." If you say it grimly it sounds as if you were drunk, and if you say it flippantly it sounds as if you were drunk. So I simply said, "No, but I read the books," and joined a

191

knot of men who were discussing whatever men discussed that many years ago.

My wife had decided to raise and sell Siamese kittens, and so Circe and Jezzie were introduced to various Siamese males. These meetings invariably resulted in nothing more productive than Oriental imprecations, insults and curses. This was just as well, since, in addition to the two cats, we also had a kennelful of French poodles —a mother poodle and her eleven puppies—and a screened-in porchful of Scottish terriers—a mother dog named Jeannie and her six puppies. The puppies of both breeds had just reached the salable age of three months when the Depression occurred and you couldn't give pets away, let alone sell them. Everybody was trying to unload everything, including saddle horses, but nobody wanted to take them.

I think it was in February, 1930, that we gave up the Silvermine house and the kennel venture and moved to New York. Five of the young poodles and all of the Scottie pups had somehow been disposed of—left in cute baskets on strangers' doorsteps, perhaps, or forced upon relatives and friends at the point of a gun or a prayer. Jeannie didn't like New York, or poodles, or cats, or anybody else, so she had been parked with my wife's sister in Westport. I had nothing to do with getting the mother poodle and her six remaining offspring to the city—it was mysteriously managed one morning by my wife and an acquaintance of ours who had agreed to go along and help, and who soon thereafter drifted or, to be precise, jumped out of our life. Since nobody else volunteered to help transport the cats to town, it was up to me. I found myself in the back seat of our car with the two cats, a checkerboard, an alarm clock, a stack of books, and a heavy cardboard mailing tube, three feet long and four inches in diameter, suitable for carrying drawings—if you're not carrying anything else. My wife drove the car, and our destination was a brownstone in West Fiftieth Street. We had rented an apartment on the top floor where the mother poodle and her six pups, now six months old and full of restlessness and destructive ingenuity, awaited us. We could hear them loudly debating something when the car stopped in front of the brownstone.

I made the mistake of trying to carry the cats and the rest of the stuff in the back seat in one armload, to my wife's dismay and to the cats' delight. They had decided by this time, it soon transpired, not to destroy me, but to humiliate me beyond rehabilitation. All this was a long time ago, but it remains sharply in my tortured memory that I had a cat and the checkerboard under one arm, and a cat and the mailing tube under the other, with the index finger of my right hand inserted in the metal ring surmounting the bell on the alarm clock. The books were somehow wedged between my chin and my crossed wrists. The metal ring fitted perfectly; that is, it was easy to get on but almost impossible to get off. Now, nothing has such an unwrapped look outdoors as an unwrapped alarm clock. There is something naked about it, something calculated to make bystanders out of passers-by, especially if it begins to ring, and this one began to ring. Uninterested passers-by suddenly became fascinated bystanders, but nobody offered to help. One or two, fearful of becoming involved in some complex racket common to the streets of New York, hastened away. My wife, halfway up the front steps when the alarm sounded, gave one quick look over her shoulder, ran the rest of the way to the front door, hastily opened it with her key, and disappeared inside. Two or three of the books I was carrying slithered to the pavement, and since the checkerboard had no latch, there was a slow dismal leakage of black and red checkers. It was at this moment that the cats decided it was time for them to dominate the shambles. One of them—Circe, I think—reached up a long graceful front leg, deftly inserted her claws into the brim of my felt hat, and slowly began to draw it down over my eyes. None of the male bystanders did anything except stare, probably figuring that this was the tertiary stage of an incurable dissolution, but a woman decided to help by picking up the books and some of the checkers and trying to pack them back onto me and my parcels of cats and still life. I didn't dare drop the cats, and I couldn't get the ringing clock off my finger, but I let everything else go, and managed somehow or other to get up the steps and reach the door, which I began kicking.

When my wife finally opened the door a few inches and peered out, she beheld a trail of books and checkers leading down to the car. The hat was in the awful pattern somewhere and the mailing tube had rolled into the gutter. The clock had mercifully stopped ringing, but the cats had begun screaming, and there is nothing this side of hell to match the screaming of Siamese cats. I think my wife and the woman Samaritan helped collect the stuff. I think I remember a cop shouting, "Break it up, now! Break it up!" When my wife and I got inside and closed the door, she took the cats away from me. I was bleeding a little from various scratches. "It isn't so good upstairs," she said. I could hear the gleeful yelping of the poodles, who seemed to think it was wonderful upstairs. My wife took the cats and left me to struggle with the clock and to reassemble the litter, some of which was inside and some of which was still out in the vestibule. The kindly woman was in the vestibule too. "Just what is it?" she asked in the tone of one who simply has to describe what she has been through when she gets home but hasn't the vaguest idea what it actually was. She gave me two checkers and I thanked her and she went away, taking my copy of *The Modern Temper* by Joseph Wood Krutch. Anyway, I hope she is the one that got it. It explains all the predicaments of modern Man except the one I got into that day, and nobody could explain that, or what was still to come.

Historicity lies so close to legend in my world that I often walk with one foot in each area, with side trips, or so my critics declare, into fantasy. This is because of my unenviable talent for stumbling from one confusion into another. Never have my confusions lain so close together, however, as the cat confusion and the dog confusion on that February day more than thirty years ago. It seems that the six young poodles in our apartment had become bored and decided to take everything apart. If you imagine that half a dozen six-month-old poodles raise only a little more than half as much deviltry as eleven would, you don't know poodles. What wasn't so good upstairs, it turned out, was the front room of the apartment where the dogs had been confined, with the hope that their mother would maintain some semblance of order in the temporary absence of human beings. She hadn't. Mother dogs lose interest in their young after they are weaned and disclaim all responsibility for what may happen, indoors or out. The young dogs had taken the phonograph apart, for one thing, and had scattered hundreds of records about the room, as if they had been frantically looking for *Moonlight Bay* and couldn't find it. Poodles do not like lettuce, mustard, and records, so the latter had not been chewed, just scattered. The phonograph had been chewed, though, wood and fabric and metal. The Ping-pong table had lost one leg to the onslaught of teeth and collapsed. The collapse would have been something to see and hear, since the table, while still upright, had held three or four paddles, a box containing a dozen balls, thirty or forty books, and an assortment of glass ash trays, all of which had been added to the jumble of records and pieces of phonograph on the floor. Poodles always listen attentively while being scolded, looking innocent, bewildered and misunderstood. As soon as the lecture was over, they wanted to know if they could take the Siamese cats apart to see what made them scream. I was all for this, but we were outvoted. I can't recall with any clarity what happened after that. Some process of defense mechanism has erased the rest of that ungainly afternoon and evening, except for the protests of a nervously disheveled gentleman who lived in the apartment below. He came up and knocked on the door and demanded to know what in the name of Heaven we were harboring and abetting. (Some people merely own dogs, but I harbor them.) "They are in transit," I said weakly. He mentioned Federal statutes, state laws, city ordinances, Christianity, common decency, the American Way of Life, and friends of his in high official positions. The young poodles and I listened attentively, all seven of us trembling slightly. The mother dog was asleep, the Siamese cats were profoundly oblivious, and my wife was indignant. What happened after that my memory refuses to divulge. I suppose I slipped away to a speakeasy, in the immemorial manner of the American husband when his household suddenly falls, or is taken, apart. I suppose the bartender who served me drinks that evening thought I was crazy when he asked me, "What do you know?" and I told him. I still wonder now and then about the husband of the woman who came home with *The Modern Temper* that evening. "Where'd you get this book?" he must have asked her, and she must have told him.

I don't know what happened to Jezzie finally, but Circe came to a violent end the following year when she sauntered too near a basket containing Jeannie's second litter of Scottish terrier pups. There was no apparent provocation and no warning, just a flash of black and a gleam of teeth, and Circe was no more. I don't think it was assault with intent to kill, but just a maternal reflex, one of the millions of incidents in the bloody pattern of prowl and pounce by means of which Nature maintains its precarious and improbable balance of survival. I am a dog

197

man, as I have confessed, and not a cat man, and as such I have always felt a curious taint of guilt about the unfortunate affair. Dick Conway never actually said so, but I think he considered me a kind of accessory before the fact. I don't know how he came to this morbid conclusion, if he did, but it worried me, and I used to lie awake thinking about Circe until, in the end, I convinced myself that she would come back to earth as a revenant and pounce on me when I was just sauntering along, unprotected and unaware. Once, during such a saunter, I banged my head against the low iron bar of a store awning and was knocked down and dazed. A passer-by helped me to my feet and I mumbled, "Did you see her? Did you see the cat?" He gave me a concerned look. "Take it easy, buddy," he said. "There wasn't any cat. You banged into that awning." He thought a moment and added, "Take a good-sized cat to knock a man down." I couldn't very well tell him, without being turned over to a cop, that I lived in fear of a Siamese cat that had passed away long ago, so I just muttered something and sauntered on, turning quickly every now and then to see if Something was following me, Something that moved swiftly and made no sound.

Then one day, about five years after Jeannie's fatal pounce, I happened to reread Clarence Day's wonderful little book called *This Simian World*. This satire on the descent of Man speculates, as almost everybody knows, on the hypothetical nature of the human being if he had descended from other creatures than the anthropoid. The funniest and sharpest chapter of this brilliant exploration deals with the human male and the human female as Cat People. As I read it I realized with a shudder what form my stealthy doom was going to take. In his cat chapter, Mr. Day imagines us all at a big party of some kind in a room with thick carpets and heavy draperies. "Someone is entering! Hush!" writes Mr. Day, and he goes on to describe a typical "lithe silken" female cat human: "Lan-

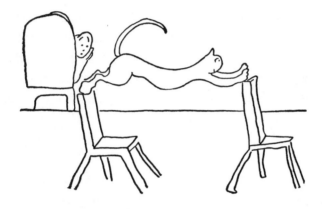

guorous, slender and passionate. Sleepy eyes that see everything. An indolent, purposeful step. An unimaginable grace. If you were *her* lover, my boy, you would learn how fierce love can be, how capricious and sudden, how hostile, how ecstatic, how violent!" I put down the book and got up and mixed myself a strong whiskey-and-soda. At least, I thought shakily, the late Circe, in contriving to bring the chapter to my attention again, had had the unimaginable grace, or perhaps merely the malicious deviltry, to forewarn me of my doom.

Several months after this dreadful revelation Jeannie

died of a surfeit of candy, a box of assorted chocolates which, I was confident, had been deliberately placed within her reach by some lithe, silken lady who walked with an indolent, purposeful step. Of course, Jeannie was a very old dog then, but she had probably spent her last years sleeping with one eye open, keeping a sharp lookout for a cat the size of a Saint Bernard, little suspecting that Circe was a woman now, dressed like other women, but a little faster of hand and foot, with slippers as soundless as velvet. They are all Pavlowas, Mr. Day had written of female cat humans, and I became wary of women dancers and of dancing in general. Once, though, off guard on a summer evening, I found myself dancing with a woman of exceedingly light step and unimaginable grace and I commented on her ability. "Oh, I'm a real Pavlowa," she said in a voice that seemed like a purr. She had sleepy eyes. I almost yelled, "Cut in on me, for God's sake, somebody! I'm dancing with Circe! I'm dancing with the cat that has sworn to kill me!" I was restrained by the sudden horrible sense that I would be seized and put away, and so I trembled through the dance until the music ended. I had not caught my partner's name, but when I demanded of my startled hostess, "Who is that Siamese cat I was dancing with?" she reassured me by saying, "You mean Betty Schwartz? She's Charley Schwartz's wife. Why?" I laughed idiotically and sighed with relief. The final irony could never be *quite* that grotesque. I was never going to be finished off by anybody named Betty. A cat human named Betty would be the reincarnation of a tabby cat, and I am only moderately afraid of tabby cats.

Clarence Day's female cat humans began to prowl my nightmares and to turn up on the corners and in the parlors of my daily life. Looking back from this distance, I can't always distinguish between the reality and the dream, the cat substance and the cat shadow. Most of the ladies, in nightmare or actuality, were possessed of strange feline agilities. One of them, although only five feet two inches tall, got a book down from a shelf too high for me to reach, and I am almost six feet two. Another wanted to discuss Carl Van Vechten and James Mason, two celebrated admirers of cats, and left me abruptly when I brought up the subject of Albert Payson Terhune. A third —oh, I must have met *her* in a dream—said, at five o'clock one afternoon in her drawing room, "Do you like tea in your cream?" I never met a Miss Graymalkin, or a Mrs. Thomas Katz who lived in a place called The Mews and tried to lure me there on the pretense of showing me her falcons. (Mews, Webster tells me, are cages for hawks.) I really did know a lady, though, who owned a Scottish terrier named Duncan and a bold female cat named Lady, whose name was lengthened to Lady Macbeth after the mysterious and violent death of Duncan. I don't know what became of this woman, but she probably knows where I am. Female cat humans, as I interpret Mr. Day, would not phone or send telegrams, since they would not believe in swift means of communication. Their swiftness lies in sudden and unexpected personal appearances.

The last, or the latest, lady of my acquaintance that I genuinely suspected of being Circe in disguise materialized in the chair next to mine about seven years ago in

Bermuda at a cocktail party which had reached midnight and was still rolling. This lady began urging me to stop arguing and to start singing, and I asked her what she wanted me to sing. My repertory consists of "Who," "Bye-Bye Blackbird," "Linger Awhile," "Do You Ever Think of Me," and "Manhattan," but what the lady wanted was a song, popular at the time, called "The Girl That I Marry." To anybody except me this song is as bland and innocuous as the satins and laces, the cologne and the gardenia with which it gently deals, and so my host and hostess and all the guests except Circe, if it was Circe, were bewildered when I leaped to my feet in the midst of the song, grabbed my hat and coat and wife, and left the party. You have probably figured what had alarmed me, now that you know all about my phobia. It was, of course, the line that goes: "I'll be sittin' next to her, and she'll purr like a kitten." After I had jammed my wife into a cab, I explained, "Maybe her purr is worse than her scratch, but she was definitely purring." My wife sighed and said simply, "We stayed too late."

At my present age, I have begun to feel that I am comparatively safe, and there are so many things besides cats and women to worry about: taxes, fission, fusion, more taxes, subversion, subcommittees, flying saucers (without cream), human beings descended from anthropoids, that persistent pain in my left shoulder, those funny sounds in the attic and in the engine of my car, my increasing blood pressure, my decreasing inventiveness, and the vast Category of Catastrophes. There I go again! This brings me right back where I started, always a good place to stop.

A note of warning, however, in conclusion: if you are a dog man who has offended a cat woman, beware of boxes of assorted chocolates that appear suddenly at your elbow without explanation. Have the chocolates analyzed by a chemist, and be sure it is a male dog chemist, and not a female cat chemist.

23

The Trouble
with Man Is Man

Man has gone long enough, or even too long, without being man enough to face the simple truth that the trouble with Man is Man. For nearly three thousand years, or since the time of Aesop, he has blamed his frailties and defects on the birds, the beasts, and the insects. It is an immemorial convention of the writer of fables to invest the lower animals with the darker traits of human beings, so that, by age-old habit, Man has come to blame his faults and flaws on the other creatures in this least possible of all worlds.

The human being says that the beast in him has been aroused, when what he actually means is that the human being in him has been aroused. A person is not pigeon-toed, either, but person-toed, and what the lady has are not crow's-feet but woman-wrinkles. It is our species, and not any other, that goes out on wildcat strikes, plays the badger game, weeps crocodile tears, sets up kangaroo courts. It is the man, and not the shark, that becomes the loan shark; the cat burglar, when caught, turns out not to be a cat but a man; the cock-and-bull story was not invented by the cock and the bull; and the male of our

species, at the height of his arrogant certainties, is mansure and not cocksure, just as, at his most put-upon, he is woman-nagged and not hen-pecked.

It is interesting to find in one dictionary that "cowed" does not come from "cow" but means, literally, "with the tail between the legs." I had naturally assumed, too, that Man blamed his quailing, or shrinking with fear, on the quail, but the dictionary claims that the origin of the verb "to quail" is uncertain. It is nice to know that "duck," meaning to avoid an unpleasant task, does not derive from our web-footed friend but from the German verb "*tauchen*," meaning "to dive." We blame our cowardice, though, on poultry, when we say of a cringing man that he "chickened out."

Lest I be suspected by friends and colleagues, as well as by the F.B.I. and the American Legion, of wearing fur or feathers under my clothing, and acting as a spy in the midst of a species that is as nervous as a man and not as a cat, I shall set down here some of the comparatively few laudatory phrases about the other animals that have passed into general usage. We say, then, that a man has dogged determination, bulldog tenacity, and is the watchdog of this or that public office, usually the Treasury. We call him lionhearted, or as brave as a lion, as proud as a peacock, as lively as a cricket, as graceful as a swan, as busy as a bee, as gentle as a lamb, and we sometimes observe that he has the memory of an elephant and works like a beaver. (Why this should make him dog-tired instead of beaver-tired I don't know.)

As I sit here, I suddenly, in my fevered fancy, get a man's-eye view, not a bird's-eye view, of a police detective snooping about a brownstone house, back in the prohibition days. He has been tipped off that the place is a blind tiger that sells white mule, or tiger sweat, and he will not believe the denials of the proprietor, one Joe, whose story sounds fishy. The detective smells a rat and begins pussyfooting around. He is sure that this is a joint in which a man can drink like a fish and get as drunk as a monkey. The proprietor may be as wise as an owl and as slippery as an eel, but the detective is confident that he can outfox him.

"Don't hound me. You're on a wild-goose chase," insists Joe, who has butterflies in his stomach, and gooseflesh. (The goose has been terribly maligned by the human being, who has even gone so far as to pretend that the German jack-boot strut is the goose step. Surely only the dog, the cat, and the bug are more derogated than the goose.) "You're as crazy as a loon," Joe quavers.

"Don't bug me," says the cop, and the bloodhound continues his search. Suddenly he flings open a door, and there stands the proprietor's current mouse, a soiled dove, as naked as a jay bird. But the detective has now ferreted out a secret panel and a cache of currency. "There must be ten thousand clams here," he says. "If you made all this fish legitimately, why do you hide it? And don't try to weasel out."

"In this rat race it's dog eat dog," the proprietor says, as he either is led off to jail or pays off the cop.

The English and American vocabularies have been vastly enlarged and, I suppose, enriched by the multitudinous figures of speech that slander and libel the lower animals, but the result has been the further inflation of the already inflated human ego by easy denigration of the other species. We have a thousand disparaging nouns applicable only to human beings, such as scoundrel, rascal, villain, scalawag, varlet, curmudgeon, and the like, but an angry person is much more apt to use, instead of one of these, such words as jackal, jackass, ape, baboon, gorilla, skunk, black sheep, louse, worm, lobster, crab, or shrimp. Incidentally, the word "curmudgeon" seems to derive from the French *"cœur méchant,"* so that an old curmudgeon is nothing worse than an old naughty heart.

The female of our species comes out of slight, slur, insult, and contumely wearing more unfavorable tags and labels than the male. The fishwife, for example, has no fishhusband. The word "shrew" derives from the name of a small

furred mammal with a malignant reputation, based on an old, mistaken notion that it is venomous. Shrews are, to be sure, made up of both males and females, but the word is applied only to the female human being. Similarly, "vixen," meaning an ill-tempered person, was originally applied to both sexes (of human beings, not of foxes), but it is now aimed only at the woman. When a man, especially a general or other leader, is called a fox, the word is usually employed in a favorable sense.

Both "shrew" and "vixen" are rarely used any more in domestic altercations. For one thing, neither implies mental imbalance, and our species is fond of epithets and invective implying insanity. The list of such slings and arrows in Roget's Thesaurus contains, of course, such expressions as "off one's rocker" and "off one's trolley," but once again the lower forms of life are accused of being "disturbed," as in "mad as a March hare," "bats," "batty," "bats in the belfry," "crazier than a bedbug," and so on. (My favorite phrase in this Roget category gets away from bugs and bats, and rockers and trolleys; it is "balmy in the crumpet.")

Every younger generation, in its time and turn, adds to our animalistic vocabulary of disparagement. A lone male at a dance is no longer a stag turned wolf when he dogs the steps of a girl; he's a bird dog. And if the young lady turns on him, she no longer snaps, "Get lost!" or "Drop dead!" but, I am told, "Clean out your cage!" Since I heard about this two years ago, however, it may well be old hat by now, having given way to something like "Put your foot back in the trap!" or "Go hide under your rock!" or "Crawl back into the woodwork!"

I am afraid that nothing I can say will prevent mankind from being unkind to catkind, dogkind, and bugkind. I find no record of any cat that was killed by care. There are no dogs where a man goes when he goes to the dogs. The bugs that a man gets out of his mechanisms, if he does get them out, are not bugs but defects caused by the ineptitude, haste, or oversight of men.

Let us all go back to counting sheep. I think that the reason for the prevalent sleeplessness of Americans must be that we are no longer counting sheep but men.

24

The Duchess and
the Bugs

It is a great moment for an Ohio writer living far from home when he realizes he has not been forgotten by the state he can't forget. He is especially happy to be so signally honored by a distinguished organization devoted to putting books on shelves instead of taking them off. The writer of humorous pieces has so much fun producing his output that he doesn't always regard it as work, and he is likely to be surprised if it is singled out for an award. He is used to being laughed at, he hopes to be laughed with, but he doesn't expect to be taken seriously, although he likes to believe Booth Tarkington was exaggerating when he said, "Sobersides looks at humor the way a duchess looks at bugs." At the same time he is proud of his trade, in spite of his moments of depression when he is convinced that he is read only by duchesses. I have heard from duchesses who suggest that I quit harping on the imaginary flaws of the American Woman and start writing a novel about her true power and glory. I reply that I may try to write such a novel—when my spirit has been broken by the American Woman's power, or transfigured by her glory.

Meanwhile, as my publishers know, I couldn't do without her. Somebody has said that Woman's place is in the wrong. That's fine. What the wrong needs is a woman's presence and a woman's touch. She is far better equipped than men to set it right. The condescending male, in his pride of strength, likes to think of the female as being "soft, soft as snow," but just wait till he gets hit by the snowball. Almost any century now Woman may lose her patience with black politics and red war and let fly. I wish I could be on earth then to witness the saving of our self-destructive species by its greatest creative force. If I have sometimes seemed to make fun of Woman, I assure you it has only been for the purpose of egging her on.

A woman practitioner of humor announced a few years ago, in an hour of despair, that humor is a shield and not a weapon. Well, the world has plenty of weapons and it can use a few shields. There used to be men among us who could brandish the shield of humor with telling effect in the now sensitive area of politics and government, giving certain Senators and Congressmen of their time a pretty good banging around. I mean such men, to name only a few, as the H. L. Mencken of an earlier and bolder day, and Finley Peter Dunne, and William Allen White, and old Ed Howe, and Ohio's unforgettable Bob Ryder. The gentle heart, thank God, is often armored in toughness, courage, and strength. The tradition of rugged and unafraid humor perpetuated by these men must not be allowed to pass into legend and limbo, out of fear and trembling. They did not invent the tradition, of course. It came over in the Mayflower, it flourished in the free American soil, it was carried westward in covered wagons, it was borne upon our battlefields as bright and inspiring as regimental colors. It has been seasick, wagon-weary, and shot full of holes, but it has always managed to keep on going.

As a matter of fact, comedy, in all its forms, including the rusty art of political satire, is used to surviving eras of stress and strain, even of fear and trembling, but it sickens in the weather of intimidation and suppression, and such a sickness could infect a whole nation. The only rules comedy can tolerate are those of taste, and the only limitations those of libel. It should be as free and respected as Lincoln's humor or Churchill's wit. It must not be mistaken for, or identified with, a man's political views, or punished for his political past. It will not bear up long under mindless picketing. We must not have guilt by talent, or guilt by profession. There has been so much banning and burning and branding that timorous writers have begun to think of writing as somehow akin to counterfeiting or forgery. One distinguished writer of comedy is reported to have promised a sub-committee of Congress that, to make up for past associations, he was going to write an anti-Communist musical comedy. Humor should never take the form of penance or of penitence. Since the nature of humor is anti-communistic, just as the nature of Communism is anti-humor, such a project would amount, in effect, to an anti-humorous musical comedy. This would be too dull and awful to contemplate, let alone to attend. I would have to be dragged to it. Our comedy should deal, in its own immemorial manner, with the American scene and the American people, without fear or favor, without guilt or groveling. There is no other form up with which, to paraphrase Sir Winston, we will ever put. Most professional writers, by the way, are happy that the Nobel prize has gone to a professional writer who says things any damned way he wants to. The thunder of his prose and the lightning of his wit have done much to clear the air for us and to illumine the way.

Let us not forget the uses of laughter or store them away in the attic. If a thing cannot endure laughter, Professor Joseph Russell Taylor used to say, it is not a good thing. He made us understand that laughter is never out of date or out of place. Dangerous men, he once said, are nourished as much by attack as they are by praise. It magnifies their importance, builds them a stately mansion on the front page, and dignifies their meanest motives and their merest shenanigans. Laughter, on the other hand, is often their undoing. It shows them up in a clear and honest light, and drives away the big distorted shadows in which they love to lurk. Many of the perils they flaunt in the shadows are real perils, but they can be dealt with better in the light. Laughter could bring many things out into the open

213

including, I should like to put in here, the true shape and purpose of our Bill of Rights. It was designated as a fortress and a sanctuary, not as a hideout.

I have no doubt that there have been a few conspiratorial writers around, but all the writers I know personally would make very incompetent conspirators. They like to do things in public, not in secret. They want everybody to know what they are up to. The night that Alexander Woollcott was fatally stricken with a heart attack he was engaged in what E. B. White described as a "public brawl," by which he meant a radio discussion panel over a nation-wide network. An elderly writer I know, a man about ten years older than I am, recently entered a New York hospital for a check-up under an assumed name. The day after he came in he asked his nurse why nobody had telephoned or sent wires and she reminded him that he had quietly entered the hospital under a pseudonym. "I know that," he said irritably, "but I thought everybody would find it out."

Some frightened sponsors and radio stations and other well-known pussycats have shown, from time to time, a phobia against anyone who has become what is known as a "controversial figure." This stupidity has struck at writers who, in this controversial country, have always been controversial persons. A controversial figure is apparently a controversial person who is not afraid to let his views be known outside his own living room. Discussion in America means dissent. We love to disagree with persons whose opinions we value, for how else are we going to make them value ours? One writer I know and admire was told by his doctors to give up coffee and controversy. He replied that he couldn't live without coffee and couldn't make a living without controversy. He might have said, with equal truth, that he couldn't live without coffee and wouldn't want to live without controversy. It is possible that this strange and unbecoming hush-hush which seems to have overtaken us is in some way responsible for the decline of humor in America. At any rate, humor flourished in the free and untrammeled twenties when, as Harold Ross once put it, humorists were a dime a dozen. There are not many left, alas, and only a handful coming up. I hope that literary humor, by which I mean humor written for newspaper, magazine, and book publication, is not dying out in the United States. It has a long and honorable tradition, but it is hanging on by aging fingertips and it needs new recruits. E. B. White once wrote: ". . . humorous writing, like poetical writing, has an extra content. It plays, like an active child, close to the big hot fire which is Truth." The devoted writer of humor will continue to try to come as close to truth as he can, even if he gets burned in the process, but I don't think he will get too badly burned. His faith in the good will, the soundness, and the sense of humor of his countrymen will always serve as his asbestos curtain.

Set in linotype Caledonia

Format by Jean Krulis

Manufactured by the Murray Printing Co. and The Haddon Craftsmen, Inc.

Published by Harper & Brothers, New York